Visual Project Management

Visual Project Management

Paul R. Williams, PMP

Think For A Change™ Publishing
Green Bay, Wisconsin USA

Ordering Information:

Special discounts are available on quantity purchases by corporations, associations, educators and others. For details, contact the publisher at the address listed below.

Discounts also exist for readers purchasing hard copies directly from Lulu Press.

U.S. trade bookstores and wholesalers: Please contact Think For A Change™ Publishing via email: VisualPMOrdering@thinkforachange.com

Legal Disclaimers:

First Printing: February 2015 via Lulu Press, Inc. and On-Demand via Amazon.com

ISBN 978-1-312-66522-4

Think For A Change™ Publishing
1678 Cady Lane
De Pere, Wisconsin 54115   United States of America

www.ThinkForAChange.com

Printing number

10 9 8 7 6 5 4 3 2 1

Dedication

For Michelle…thank you for your patience, your willingness to listen without judgment, your gentle nudges in the right direction and your encouragement to take calculated risks. This thing we call life and a career has been a wonderful, interesting and blessedly rewarding journey thus far, and I wouldn't change a single minute. Here's to the second half!

*   *   *

"If you don't build your own dream, someone else will hire you to help build theirs." – Tony A. Gaskins, Jr.

*   *   *

"If there's a book that you want to read, but it hasn't been written yet, then you must write it and share it with the world." – Toni Morrison

Contents

Acknowledgements..**xi**

Introduction..**xiii**

Visual Thinking Overview...**1**

Visual Project Management 3
An Introduction to Visual Management Concepts 7
The 'Data Visualization' Concept......................................*7*
The 'Visual Thinking' Concept...*10*

Visual Thinking Tools for Project Management..............**13**

Mind Mapping..15
Process Mapping 21
Storyboarding 25
Root Cause Analysis...31
Charting, Diagramming & Graphing.....................................37
Drawing / Sketching 47
Wireframes & Use Cases..53

Visual Project Reporting...**57**

Earned Value Analysis 59
Earned Value Analysis (General).....................................*59*
Earned Value Analysis (with Tolerance Limiting).............*64*
Dashboards 69
Road Maps..81
Lean Concepts - Kanban 87
Agile Concepts – Scrum Visuals 95
Scrum Overview..*95*
Scrum Task Board..*97*
Scrum Sprint Burn-Down Chart......................................*100*
Infographics...103

Visual Project Collaboration..**111**

Project War Room 113
Project "Science Fair" 119
Visual Project Displays 123
Project Display Walls..*123*

Project Showcase or Exhibition *125*
Project Flight Planning and Status Boards............................*129*
3D Project Environments *134*
Project Social Media...137
Gamification in Project Management...145

Epilogue **153**

About The Author **155**

Bibliography..**157**

Endnotes **165**

Table of Figures & Charts

Figure 1 - Simple Mind Map Example 16
Figure 2 - Sample Sub-Project Mind Map 18
Figure 3 - Sample Project Management Mind Map 19
Figure 4 - Basic Process Flow Chart 23
Figure 5 - Basic Cross-Functional (Swim lane) Flow Chart 23
Figure 6 - Storyboard Scene Template 27
Figure 7 - Complete Scene Card 27
Figure 8 - Card Sequence View..28
Figure 9 - Example Storyboard Wall..28
Figure 10 - 5 Whys Technique 33
Figure 11 - Ishikawa (Fishbone) Diagram..34
Figure 12 - Failure Mode & Effect Analysis.....................................35
Figure 13 - Example of a Bar Chart 39
Figure 14 - Example of a Line Chart..39
Figure 15 - Example of a Pie Chart..40
Figure 16 - Example of a Radar Chart..40
Figure 17 - Example of a Bubble Chart..41
Figure 18 - Example of a Waterfall Chart 41
Figure 19 - Example of a Flow Chart..42
Figure 20 - Example of a Venn Diagram 42
Figure 21 - Example of a Histogram 43
Figure 22 - Example of a Gantt Chart 44
Figure 23 - Example of a Project Network Diagram / PERT Chart...44
Figure 24 - Sample Sketch – Buyer Purchase Experience 50
Figure 25 - Sample Doodle – Strategic Horizon 50
Figure 26 - Webpage Wireframe Drawing Example...........................54
Figure 27 – Use Case Example 55
Figure 28 - Simple Earned Value Chart Example 61
Figure 29 - Sample Control Chart 64
Figure 30 - Sample Earned Value Chart with Tolerance Limits........65
Figure 31 - Common Dashboard Pictographs 70
Figure 32 - Sample Status Report Dashboard 73
Figure 33 - Sample Project Approval Dashboard...............................74
Figure 34 – Sample Program Level Dashboard 75
Figure 35 – Sample Project Scorecard Dashboard 76
Figure 36 - Sample Project Health Check Dashboard........................77

Figure 37 - Sample Portfolio Metric Tracking Dashboard................78
Figure 38 - Example Strategic Road Map 83
Figure 39 - Sample Project Portfolio Road Map 85
Figure 40 - Simple Kanban Board....................................90
Figure 41 - Advanced Kanban Board...................................91
Figure 42 - Photo of Actual Kanban Board for Knowledge Work.....92
Figure 43 - Simple Scrum Task Board Example......................98
Figure 44 - Advanced Scrum Task Board Example 98
Figure 45 - Sprint Burndown Chart Data Example 100
Figure 46 - Sprint Burndown Chart Example.........................101
Figure 47 - Infographic Design Balance 104
Figure 48 - Example Infographic 107
Figure 49 - Sample Project Communication Infographic...............108
Figure 50 - Infographic-Based Project Milestone Plan 109
Figure 51 - Example of a Project War Room 115
Figure 52 - Project War Room Example 117
Figure 53 - Example of a Corporate Project "Science Fair"............120
Figure 54 - Photo from 3M "15% Time" Showcase Event 122
Figure 55 - Project Display Wall Example............................124
Figure 56 – Static Project Showcase Example 125
Figure 57 - Project Exhibit Example 126
Figure 58 – Event-Based Project Exhibition Example 127
Figure 59 – 3M Innovation Center in Dubai, UAE 128
Figure 60 - DuPont Innovation Center in Moscow, Russia.............128
Figure 61 - Sample Flight Plan Templates 129
Figure 62 - Project Management Process Checklist Example 1.......130
Figure 63 - Project Management Process Checklist Example 2.......131
Figure 64 - Typical Flight Path Steps................................132
Figure 65 - Flight Path Aligned to Project Processes.....................132
Figure 66 - Actual Project Usage of the Flight Path Concept 133
Figure 67 - Project Status Board – Simple 133
Figure 68 - Project Status Board – Advanced 134
Figure 69 - Project Status Board Example - Sophisticated 134
Figure 70 - The Social Media Spectrum................................138
Figure 71 - Sample Gamification User Profile..........................146
Figure 72 - Sample Gamification Leaderboard 147
Figure 73 - SimulTrain®10 PM Simulation Software Screenshot...150

Acknowledgements

Ultimately, the seed for this work was planted about seven or eight years ago while I was working as a senior project leader at a former employer. Sometime around the midpoint of my tenure there, I was invited to participate in a kaizen event (they were all the rage at the time) to improve the project management process. During a brainstorming exercise on how to communicate project status in a more executive-friendly manner, someone mentioned that a certain project manager, not in the PMO at the time, was consistently receiving high praise from executive leadership for his ability to deliver results and communicate effectively at their level. It turned out that this project manager was managing projects with far greater detail than anyone else in the organization. His projects were managed primarily on cost, balanced to the penny and brutally honest in the presentation of the project metrics. Most notable, however, were the project status binders he published, full of colorful graphs, charts and other data visualizations that allowed executives to fully and quickly understand the health of the projects they were sponsoring. In fact, it wasn't uncommon to see executives walking around with these binders under their arm as they moved from meeting to meeting. It was then that I realized the tremendous impact and potential that data visualization had in project management and leadership success. That project manager, Kent Holzworth, eventually became EPMO Director for the organization, not to mention my boss and mentor. Thanks to his leadership and guidance, I have had a very successful project management career following his model of presenting project facts, in an easy to understand manner, so decisions can be made quickly and with high confidence.

Also, special thanks to the many people who took time out of their busy lives to help proofread the early drafts, offer suggestions on edits, ensure I was attributing all of the quotes and usage of graphics and photographs correctly, and for simply playing the role of "editor" as I was focused on trying to get these concepts down on paper.

For those who volunteered to review the final draft of this work and provide professional feedback, along with honest reviews and recommendations, I owe each and every one of you a debt of gratitude and thanks.

Finally, I want to recognize the many people who have attended my conference and workshop presentations regarding this topic and have shared feedback and encouraging remarks. Many of your suggestions have found their way into this work! And to those with whom I have had the pleasure of working directly within this visual project management niche over the course of the past decade, your ideas and recommendations have refined and improved the concepts, tools and thought leadership that you now see in use across the globe today. Thank you!

Introduction

My journey into this unique niche of the project management world came about as a result of two experiences, one of a more general nature and one quite specific. As anyone in the innovation management field can tell you, the best innovations typically come about from the combination of two widely disparate ideas. Combining visual thinking techniques with project management discipline has always seemed to be a natural fit to me. But it wasn't until I started searching for other best practices of applying visual methods to project management that I realized there was virtually no thought leadership on this topic outside of some agile software development methodologies.

The first generalized influence that visual thinking had on my project management career stems from my life-long passion and professional experience in creative problem solving, ideation and innovation management. Within the unstructured realm of the "fuzzy front end" of innovation, tools like mind-maps, sketches and infographics rule the day. These visual-based tools help to generate, visualize, structure and classify ideas for further examination.

In the slightly more controlled processes of the "messy back end," where ideas and concepts become tangible, visual thinking tools organize the workflows, help with decision-making and bring structure to a traditionally unstructured process. Visual management at this level improves stakeholder communication, facilitates robust cross-functional collaboration and brings clarity to complex processes and task lists.

The primary key influence, however, that visual thinking has had in my project management practice resulted from a very specific episode of workplace rebellion. I was working as a Senior Program Manager for a financial services company at the time. The organization had a well-defined project management process and methodology. Some would say the process was a bit too well defined. The use of templates was not only encouraged, they were required. Teams of project auditors would occasionally troll through project documentation folders to verify that the templates were not only being used, but were not modified in any meaningful way. Consistency and conformance were the mantra.

As in most organizations with formal Project Management Offices, new concepts that were green-lighted for project initiation from the executive leadership ranks or through the budget appropriations process were asked to prepare a formal "Request for Project Approval" document. This document artifact came in the form of a Microsoft PowerPoint® "slide deck" and would be presented to the Project Approval Committee, made up of executive team members with titles like CFO, COO, CIO and the like. The RPA deck was a well-choreographed document with strict rules for what could and could not be included. Minimally encompassing eight pages of "required" information, some legendary decks tipped the scales at twenty to thirty pages of extraneous information contained within the appendix of the document. Anyone who put material after the "Appendix" title slide knew that the odds of any information actually being read post-meeting were a loser's bet.

As a Senior Program Manager, my role included frequent trips to the Project Approval Committee for the presentation of project approval requests. In this role, I would build deck after deck after deck, each one staying within the PMO prescribed guidelines. Because these were C-level executives, the date and time of each Project Approval Committee meeting was set well in advance. The Project Leadership Team's preparation time, however, would typically begin two to three weeks ahead of the actual meeting.

This process would start by taking selections of data from various project initiation documents such as the project charter, the budget worksheet or project scope definition document, and dropping them into the scripted sections of the deck. A series of meetings would be scheduled to review and edit each page and then review it again. Lengthy meetings with Finance were held to make sure the costs and benefits were accurately calculated. Somewhere in the lead up to the document submittal deadline, some crisis would arise causing more meetings to be held and edits to be made. Numbers would change at least two or three times. No one wanted to endure the verbal tirade that the discovery of an erroneous figure would inevitably spark. Stories of project managers being dressed down for not having accurate information were legendary among the PMO...true or not.

The presentation to the Project Approval Committee essentially walked through the RPA deck page by page. First, the agenda was reviewed. Next was an overview of the project and its objectives. This was followed by the business need or driver for why the project should be done. Depending on the type of project being implemented, a technical solution page was usually provided next. On the fifth page, the project's benefits, both hard and soft were discussed. The next page included the high-level project schedule, which was only a "shot in the dark" at this point as no real project planning had been done. Finally, on page seven, came the project budget and cost information. Usually presented as a "level zero" estimate (a range of plus or minus fifty percent), this figure, no matter how much the project manager argued, would forever be etched in stone and serve as the "Sword of Damocles" under which the project team would operate for the remainder of the effort.

After going through this process a few times, I began to notice a pattern of behavior among the committee members, not only during my presentations, but also throughout all of the Request for Approval presentations that would occur during the meeting. Each presentation would start out about the same, and get at least as far as the overall business need section. After about five minutes into each and every presentation, however, at least one committee member would check their phone or open up their tablet. Another would start to page through the printed deck. This would often lead others to also begin leafing through the deck. The rustle of paper shuffling would become quite noticeable at about the same time in each and every presentation. The presenter, myself included, would continue on with his or her prepared remarks, trying not to get distracted by the lack of attention being paid.

This would go on until a quorum of the committee members reached the place in the deck where the first dollar sign appeared, at which time one of them would interrupt the carefully scripted remarks and begin asking questions about estimated costs, projected savings, return on investment, payback period or resource commitments. No matter how important the project team thought any additional non-financial information remained in the presentation, the balance of the meeting time allocated would remain solely focused on the financial points.

After going through this overly dramatic and stressful ritual a number of times, I made a commitment to try something new. I knew that going "off-script" on my own was potentially a career-limiting decision. The alternative, however, of trying to secure change of an entrenched process through the PMO was likely a long and fruitless battle. Still, I felt compelled to find a more effective and efficient way to communicate what the steering committee members most wanted to know. If they consistently flipped through each and every deck until they reached the financial information, why was it buried on page seven of the deck?

What was needed was a way to keep the committee members from flipping around the deck while the presentation was being made. But how do you stop people from flipping ahead through a stack of paper? That's when I remembered something I had previously used during my consulting work in innovation management. When faced with the problem of presenting a lot of information in a small space, the one page infographic immediately came to mind.

An infographic is a representation of rich visual content that is presented in a way to quickly and clearly convey a mix of complex data and information. It displays only the most pertinent information on a single page. The following is a representation of the infographic that I developed for that liberating first act of process defiance.

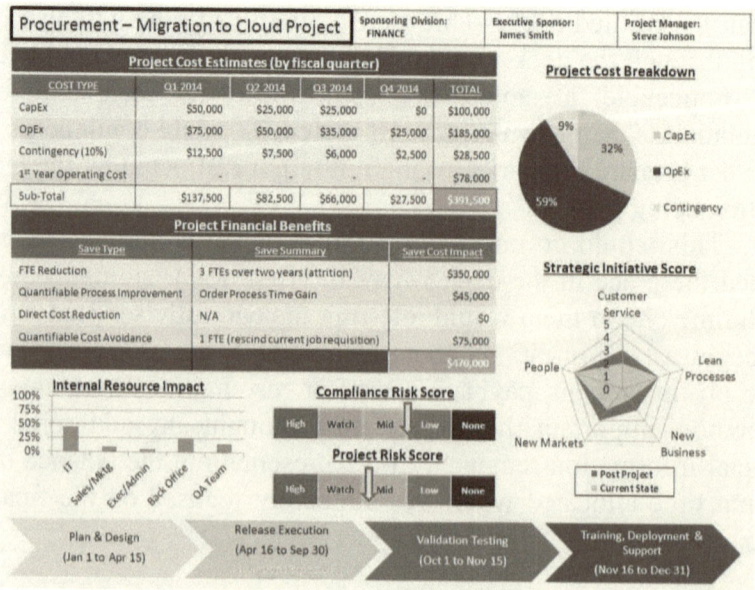

I'll admit that I wasn't a complete process deviant, as I did draft the required RPA deck for this specific project and submitted it ahead of time for presentation at the review meeting. I also gave a "heads-up" to both my Project Leadership Team and the Director of the PMO, all of whom encouraged me to try this new concept. When the time came to review our project and the full deck was being handed out, I also passed around this one-page infographic and mentioned that it essentially covered all of the pertinent information we were going to discuss. While I had hoped for a positive reaction, I was surprised by the instantaneous and overwhelmingly supportive response from each and every one of the committee members.

In a nutshell, the committee members shared that this was something they had been requesting for some time, with the hope that it would help speed up the approval meetings and cut right to the more salient points of what they considered important in order to approve or defer a new project. A few members provided additional feedback on what alternative information would be more helpful, while others shared that some data on my infographic could be dropped in favor of the more useful proposed additions. They unanimously requested that the PMO transition to this "one-pager" view over the course of the next two meetings.

In reality, it took a few extra meetings to get the new one-page format details ironed out, but the organization did eventually get to the point where the approval meetings became more effective, efficient and focused. Leadership satisfaction with the process was greatly improved. However, the main positive impact in the process changeover was realized in preparation time and effort. While meetings were still necessary to organize the text of the document, make sure the financials were correct and ensure that the information being conveyed was accurate, the actual amount of preparation time was reduced drastically.

This action ignited follow-on discussions around what other impacts visual thinking tools and techniques could have, not only in the project management practice area, but also in business processes, strategic planning, marketing approaches and other corners of the organization far from the project approval process. It also became my personal "call to action" that eventually led to this book. I began studying anything and everything I could find about visual thinking and how it could be applied to project management discipline.

Quite honestly, visual thinking techniques have simply become a collection of tools that make up my complete professional "tool box." It doesn't matter if I'm wearing my project manager hat, or my innovation manager hat, or my resource manager hat or my strategic business leader hat; the tools available to me are the same. When confronted with a problem to solve or a situation to lead, I simply sift through my toolbox for the best tool to use, regardless of its more traditional application. For example:

- If I need to quickly capture the breakdown of a stream of work, I'll bring up my mind mapping software
- If I have an issue come up on project, I'll turn to my Issue Log template
- If the team needs to analyze root cause on that issue, I'll facilitate a working session using the 5 Why's process
- On just about every project, I'll leverage the earned value formula and display actual status trending on an EVA graph

In essence, I'll assess each situation uniquely and apply the right tool for the job rather than falling victim to Maslow's old adage, "If all you have is a hammer, every problem looks like a nail.[1]"

My hope for the project management professional reading this work is an increased awareness for, and expanded knowledge of, the vast array of visual thinking tools available that can be leveraged as part of their professional practice. It is also my wish that this professional development include the creation and maintenance of a problem solving "tool box," along with the understanding of what tools are better suited to solve which problems. Enjoy!

Paul R. Williams, PMP

---

[1] Abraham H. Maslow (1966). The Psychology of Science. p. 15.

Visual Thinking Overview

Visual Project Management

In today's time-compressed and lean business culture, busy executive sponsors and key project stakeholders simply do not have the luxury of time to digest a verbose, three-page project status report on a weekly basis. Likewise, their double-booked calendars can no longer support attending status briefing meetings that simply regurgitate information that is otherwise available in alternative forms. Conscious decisions must constantly be made by project leadership regarding when to be engaged and when to simply monitor progress. Based on this new reality, managing project-based work in a "business as usual" fashion is no longer a feasible option.

Time-honored, structured processes and document-laden approaches to managing projects are rapidly being left behind in favor of more agile-based methods. Lengthy, paper-based project artifacts take significant time and effort to both generate and consume. Established waterfall and command-and-control structures no longer address the new, innovative manner in which work is now being conducted and managed.

Taking cues from the productivity gains experienced using lean manufacturing approaches in the 1980s, and the re-birth of incremental software development methods in the 1990s, led to the 2001 formation of the *Manifesto for Agile Software Development*[2], better known simply as the Agile Manifesto. This movement wasn't created to eliminate software development approaches or project management methodology, but to make them more balanced, less rigid, lighter in documentation and fluid in planning.

Agile-based methods of managing projects have started to become entrenched in even the most conservative industries like financial services, insurance and healthcare. Self-managed teams are beginning to replace top-down structures. Time-boxed "chunks" of work, rather than start-to-finish individual task sequencing, has allowed for increased velocity of completing deliverables. Focusing on the most important work, versus the work that is simply next in line, has produced more functional products.

Make no mistake, however, that traditional project management methodologies still play an important and valuable role in executing upon the strategic visions of many organizations and their products/services. The focus shift on 'doing the right thing' as compared to 'doing the thing right' has pushed both traditional and agile methods forward in a positive way. Cross-pollination from a number of different methodologies has led to an impressive diversity of custom approaches dedicated to finding the most efficient and effective way getting the work done.

One of many new customized approaches gaining traction in project management circles today is a concept that presents project-related information in a visual, often graphical, form to improve clarity, visibility and understanding of the scope or execution of the effort. This "Visual Project Management" approach serves as an additional tool for project management professionals to provide:

- At-a-glance views of project status
- Real-time project status tracking
- Real-time issue management and resolution status
- Data rich environments for better decision making

The key benefit of this new approach is speed. Critical project information can be produced, replicated and digested in more effective and efficient ways. Another advantage visual project management provides is that the information is delivered in such a way that anyone can consume it at a time, place and manner that is convenient to them.

Traditionally, project information distribution has been based on "push" methods of communication. In push-based communication, the sender, typically the project manager, decides the "who, how, what and when" regarding project information flow. This type of information is typically delivered in the form of e-mails, status reports, project status meetings, conference calls and in some cases, instant or text-based messaging. The recipient doesn't really get a choice regarding whether they receive the communication or not. Nor do they have a say in what format it is designed or delivered.

Alternatively, more and more information is being made available electronically, meant to be digested when the recipient has the time to review it. In this "pull-based" form of communication, information is simply posted to a common location, akin to a bulletin board or document library. The recipient chooses what information they want to receive and when they want to access it. Most importantly, it creates the opportunity for the project manager and the project stakeholders to have a conversation about what information and specific data points are most important to them. Then, leveraging any number of visual thinking tools, the project manager can design the format that most clearly and efficiently serves stakeholder needs.

For visualizing project management specific information, three main categories of tools exist, each with a number of specific techniques or approaches, which increase project stakeholder understanding and clarity surrounding complex project data:

1. Visual Thinking Tools that Support Project Management
   a. Mind Mapping
   b. Process Mapping
   c. Storyboarding
   d. Root Cause Analysis
   e. Charting, Diagramming and Graphing
   f. Drawing and Sketching
   g. Wireframes and Use Cases
2. Visual Project Reporting Tools
   a. Earned Value Analysis
   b. Dashboards
   c. Road Maps
   d. Lean Concepts – Kanban
   e. Agile Concepts - Scrum
   f. Infographics
3. Visual Project Collaboration Tools
   a. Project War Room
   b. Project Science Fair
   c. Project Display Wall

d. Project Collaboration Wall
e. Project Flight Status Board
f. Project Social Media
g. 3D Project Environments
h. Project Gamification

Each of these tools is explored in-depth further along in this work, including examples of where each tool is most appropriate during which project management phase or activity. Before jumping directly into the tools, however, perhaps a more high-level overview of general visual management and thinking concepts is appropriate.

An Introduction to Visual Management Concepts

The 'Data Visualization' Concept

Today's global environment is becoming increasingly more complex and interconnected at an almost incomprehensible rate. One critical by-product of that complexity and interconnectedness is something innocuously called "big data." This "data" is generated continuously, accumulating exponentially with each passing millisecond. Raw data, in and of itself, is practically useless without proper context. However, when the data is collected, stored, "mined" and then viewed with the appropriate perspective, it becomes one of the most valued and sought after resources in the modern world.

Similarly, as the pace of change accelerates, and as business challenges become more multi-faceted and complex, many leaders are increasingly finding it difficult to visualize and organize the chaos created among the myriad of data points, environmental and market factors, or influences, both internal and external. Witness the typical strategic planning meetings where, after lengthy discussion around complex organizational concepts and bulleted charts, the situation devolves hopelessly into utter confusion and frustration. Only after someone, out of sheer desperation of attempting to get his or her point across, finally draws out the concept on a whiteboard or easel pad, does the discussion finally become productive again.

So what is this lens of visual perspective that allows a seemingly meaningless stream of complex data to become a desired commodity? It is a concept known as Data Visualization and the corresponding discipline of Visual Thinking.

Data visualization refers to the technique of communicating complex data or information by converting it into a visual object or graphical representation in order to aid in visual processing and comprehension. Effective visualization makes data more understandable and usable for analysis and communication.

One of the early pioneers of data visualization theory is Edward Tufte, who authored the seminal book on this topic, *The Visual Display of Quantitative Information*. In the book, Mr. Tufte defines graphical displays, and principles for effective graphical display, in the following passage: "*Excellence in statistical graphics consists of complex ideas communicated with clarity, precision and efficiency. Graphical displays should:*

- *Show the data*
- *Induce the viewer to think about the substance rather than about methodology, graphic design, the technology of graphic production or something else*
- *Avoid distorting what the data have to say*
- *Present many numbers in a small space*
- *Make large data sets coherent*
- *Encourage the eye to compare different pieces of data*
- *Reveal the data at several levels of detail, from a broad overview to the fine structure.*
- *Serve a reasonably clear purpose: description, exploration, tabulation or decoration.*
- *Be closely integrated with the statistical and verbal descriptions of a data set.*

Graphics reveal data. Indeed graphics can be more precise and revealing than conventional statistical computations."[3]

In recent years, data visualization has become an active area of research, teaching and development. Scholars and practitioners in the field have even begun to branch out into a number of specialty areas:

Informational Graphics are graphical visual representations of information, data or knowledge intended to present complex information quickly and clearly. They can improve cognition by utilizing graphics to enhance the human visual system's ability to see patterns and trends.[4]

Visual Literacy is the ability to interpret, negotiate, and make meaning from information presented in the form of an image, extending the meaning of literacy, which commonly signifies interpretation of written or printed text. Visual literacy is based on the idea that pictures can be "read" and that meaning can be communicated through a process of reading pictorial information.[5]

Exploratory Data Analysis is an approach in statistical modeling for analyzing data sets to summarize their main characteristics, often with visual methods.[6]

Common tools used in Data Visualization are:
- Charts
- Diagrams
- Drawings
- Graphs
- Ideograms
- Pictograms
- Data Plots
- Schematics
- Tables
- Technical Drawings or Illustrations
- Maps or Cartograms

The results generated by the use of these tools serve as feedback for conducting certain analytical tasks such as depicting cause and effect, discovering the ratio of one data set against another, showing trends or cycles, revealing anomalies or rare events in repeatable processes, discovering correlations between two or more sets of data and/or ranking categories of data.

One of the reasons that the conversion of data into graphical renderings is such a key contributor to understanding complex processes and concepts stems from the fact that the human mind is naturally designed to more easily process information in the form of pictures. This concept is also known as Visual Thinking.

The 'Visual Thinking' Concept

At its core, visual thinking is the natural process of how the human mind captures, processes and understands the visual world. True "visual thinking," or the phenomenon of seeing and processing words as pictures and/or images, is common in approximately 60%–65% of the general population.[7] This means that fully two-thirds of those with whom a person regularly interacts with, both personally and professionally, will process information and communication that is transformed into images within their mind. Something to think about when formulating the best way to communicate an intended message or concept!

While it seemingly does take longer for the brain to process words vs. pictures, the time is actually negligible. In fact, reading itself is a form of visual thinking in that humans see letters as individual pictures and words as patterns. Unfortunately, the public's common knowledge of this concept stems from the following well-debunked internet meme that began circulation sometime in 2003:

> *"Aoccdrnig to a rscheearch at Cmabrigde Uinervtisy, it deosn't mttaer in waht oredr the ltteers in a wrod are, the olny iprmoetnt tihng is taht the frist and lsat ltteer be at the rghit pclae. The rset can be a toatl mses and you can sitll raed it wouthit porbelm. Tihs is bcuseae the huamn mnid deos not raed ervey lteter by istlef, but the wrod as a wlohe."[i]*

Some commonly cited visual thinking statistics however, have actually been proven to be true. For instance, scientific study conducted by molecular biologist, Dr. John Mediana has shown that there are more

---

[i] Many popular and commonly repeated "facts" of how the mind captures and processes visual information are frequently distributed as fun "did you know" pieces on the internet. For a great review regarding the validity of these "facts," the author refers the reader to ImageThink.net (http://www.imagethink.net/imagethink-2/true-or-falsevisuals-superior-medium)

neurons in the human brain dedicated to vision than the other four senses (touch, smell, hearing and taste) **combined**![8]

Additionally, a 1999 research paper titled, *Integrating Vision with the Other Senses[9]*, written by neurodevelopmental optometrist Dr. Merrill Bowan cites a 1957 study conducted by R.S.Fixot *"that upwards of 50% of the neural tissue is devoted to vision directly or indirectly. And almost incredibly, two-thirds of the electrical activity of the brain is devoted to vision when the eyes are open. Two of three billion firings per second are from the visual sense."*[10]

Since science has proven that the human mind is "pre-wired" for visual thought processes, and since the majority of the population already thinks and learns in terms of visual objects, the question becomes, how to enhance this natural ability for the benefit of an organization or to encourage the entrepreneurial spirit? The answer is the formation of core visual thinking principles for learning and organizational development.

Visual thinking, as an area of academic focus, is the consolidation of study in neuroscience, art, storytelling, information design, visual perception, color theory, shape/pattern recognition and graphic design. It extends beyond the "black and white" world of spreadsheet grids and word processing rules. It is a discipline that leverages a myriad of tools to bring ideas and concepts developed in the mind, out into the external world for further examination and testing. It seeks to bring clarity to complex concepts and brings truth to the adage that "a picture is worth a thousand words." Seeing is not only believing...seeing is understanding!

One of the common misconceptions around visual thinking is that it is solely an individual activity. While actual thought-processing is an individual effort, the facilitation and encouragement of extracting those thoughts, ideas and concepts out into a visual format can be a group-based activity.

Many organizations underestimate the strategic importance and bottom line impact that visual thinking can bring to the workplace. Tactical, facilitated visual thinking activities can bring significant positive impact within any business function and has even experienced a renaissance as of late from a number of different organizational sources:

- Strategic Management
  o Vision & Mission Development
  o Scenario Planning
    ▪ What If? Analysis

- o   Organizational/Strategic Road Map Development
- Product Management
  - o   New Product Development
  - o   Target Market Assessments
  - o   Product Lifecycle Management
  - o   Product Road Map Development
  - o   Product Documentation
  - o   Prototyping
- Marketing & Communications
  - o   Sales & Marketing Campaign Management
  - o   Customer "Day In The Life" (DITL) Analysis
  - o   Customer Use Case Development
- Finance
  - o   Forecasting & Backcasting Analysis
  - o   Risk Analysis & Mitigation Planning
  - o   Financial Modeling
- Project Management
  - o   End User, Business and/or System Requirements
  - o   Project Timeline and Road Map Development
  - o   Project Communications Management

As the speed of business continues to increase, and as focus on an ever growing number of data points is needed to keep business execution in control, new and innovative tools and techniques will be required to help busy executives make efficient and effective decisions on where to invest money and resources. Today, the visualization of data and complex processes serve those needs. By building upon this foundation, thought leaders of the visual thinking and management space will bring new and meaningful methods to the future of work.

Visual Thinking Tools for Project Management

Mind Mapping

By far the most popular visual thinking tool in use today is Mind Mapping. While modern day credit for this "hub-and-spoke," or spider diagramming, technique is often credited to popular British psychology author and television personality Tony Buzan, archeological evidence has been discovered that traces its usage as far back as the 3rd century A.D.. Buzan is, however, credited with coining the term "mind map" as part of his 1974 BBC TV program and companion book series titled, *Use Your Head*.

A mind map is simply a diagram used to visually organize information. The majority of mind maps are simple, handwritten documents used to capture notes, ideas, thoughts and comments during meetings or planning sessions. Many software packages have also been developed to convert handwritten notes into a more presentable format or to facilitate the capture of ideas in real-time. Mind mapping uses specific visual imagery and parent-child relationships to capture and organize strings of thought. Each thought captured is likely to trigger additional associations and thought patterns, spurring yet another string of thought.

At the center of the map is the central theme, or the base concept that is being considered. Radiating out from the central theme are the major ideas directly related to the central theme. Additional sub-ideas can branch out from the major ideas as needed to organize the concepts and their relationships. A simple mind map is shown here to help the reader visualize these relationships.

Figure 1 - Simple Mind Map Example

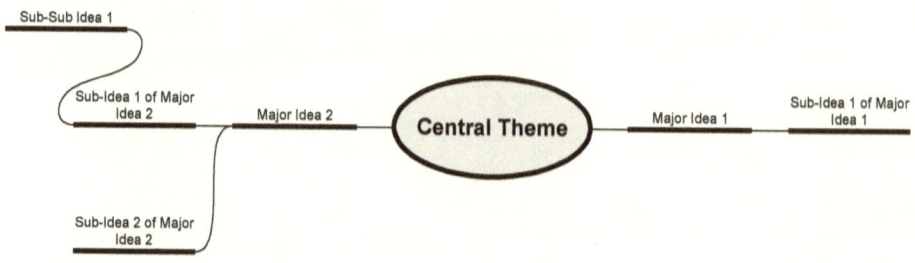

Images, thought (word) fragments, notes and other representations associated with the central theme or ideas can also added to the mind map to trigger additional thought and idea paths. The combination of a radial, tree-like organization of thoughts, along with pictorial cues sketched on the map, serve as a true "brain dump" on the topic at hand.

Mind mapping is applicable for many applications across both personal and professional situations such as planning out a novel, organizing educational concepts, note taking, personal and organizational brainstorming, creative problem solving and any number of additional use cases. Research also shows that mind mapping increases the effectiveness and efficiency of concept retention, comprehension and quality of ideas generated.[11] [12] [13]

According to Buzan[14] [15], there are some best practice guidelines to follow in creating useful mind maps:

1. Start in the center of a blank page turned sideways (landscape)
   a. Provides the brain plenty of room to think in all directions
2. Use an image or picture for the central idea
   a. Sparks the idea generation process using the "pictures are worth a thousand words" concept
3. Use different colors throughout the mind map
   a. Color adds life and organization to the map
4. Connect the main branches to the central idea and second- and third-level branches to the main branches
   a. This provides linkage, context and association to the map
5. Make the branches curved, not straight lines
   a. Straight lines are boring
6. Use one key word per line

   a. Single keywords or concepts allow for broader branching
      of additional concepts
7. Use images throughout the mind map
   a. Each additional image is also worth a thousand words

Employing the mind mapping approach within the world of
project management makes absolute logical sense. Project managers are
tasked with the organization of large amounts of project-related data
points and ordered lists. While these data points, lists and other
collections of information are all related to the overall management of a
particular project, they are not all structured, classified or utilized in the
same manner. Because mind maps lend themselves so easily to
organizing different categories of data and information quickly, orderly
and visually, they have become an incredibly popular tool among project
management professionals and provide additional key benefits that
include:

1. An ideal framework for documenting Work Breakdown
   Structures
2. Easily documenting in-scope and out-of-scope items
3. Organizing project resources, roles and responsibilities
4. Organizing project notes in a centralized location
5. Listing key project milestones, deliverables or other goals set
   by the project stakeholders
6. Serving as a "parking lot" for staging meeting agenda topics,
   change requests, scope clarifications and other discussion
   points for future use or reference

The sample mind map in Figure 2 represents a visualization of a
singular process within a larger web-based application development
project. The process identified as the central theme is an "Online Web
Store". Note how the individual components of the process (Screen
Layout, Security, et al.) branch into logical sub-components. Beyond
those, additional work flows or specific tasks are identified. Project
Managers can use this tool to organize these component streams of work,
or summary tasks, within the Work Breakdown Structure or Project Task
Plan document artifacts.

Figure 2 - Sample Sub-Project Mind Map

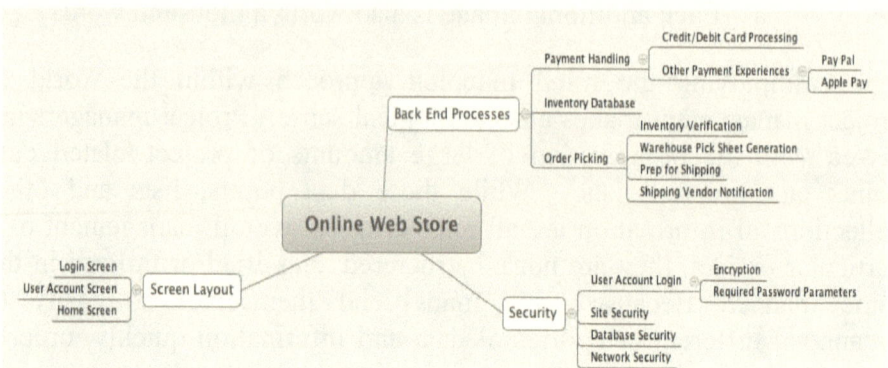

While mind maps are typically used on projects at the summary task or deliverable level, entire project efforts have been managed using nothing but a mind map. They eliminate the rigid limitations imposed by more traditional project management tools like Gantt charts or earned value calculations. Even the usage of process maps, another commonly used visual management tool discussed in the next chapter, has a tendency to guide people into linear, well-ordered thinking. Mind maps, on the other hand, encourage non-linear, radiant thinking.

Mind maps are also very useful in briefing new team members on the background of the project. When a new team member is assigned to the project, the map will provide a picture of the overall project goals, bringing them up to speed very quickly. They can instantly see, via the graphical overview of the tasks and other pertinent project information, how all of the data points on the map interrelate, including importance and impact, within the greater scheme of the overall project.

New team members can then be familiarized with their assigned project role and responsibilities, giving them a better understanding of what and how they will contribute to the team and the project. Because of the easy to understand overview, team members will very quickly "buy-in" on the project goals, whether they are coming in at the start of the project or part way through. They can see exactly where they fit in, why they are needed and how they can contribute.

Figure 3 - Sample Project Management Mind Map[16]

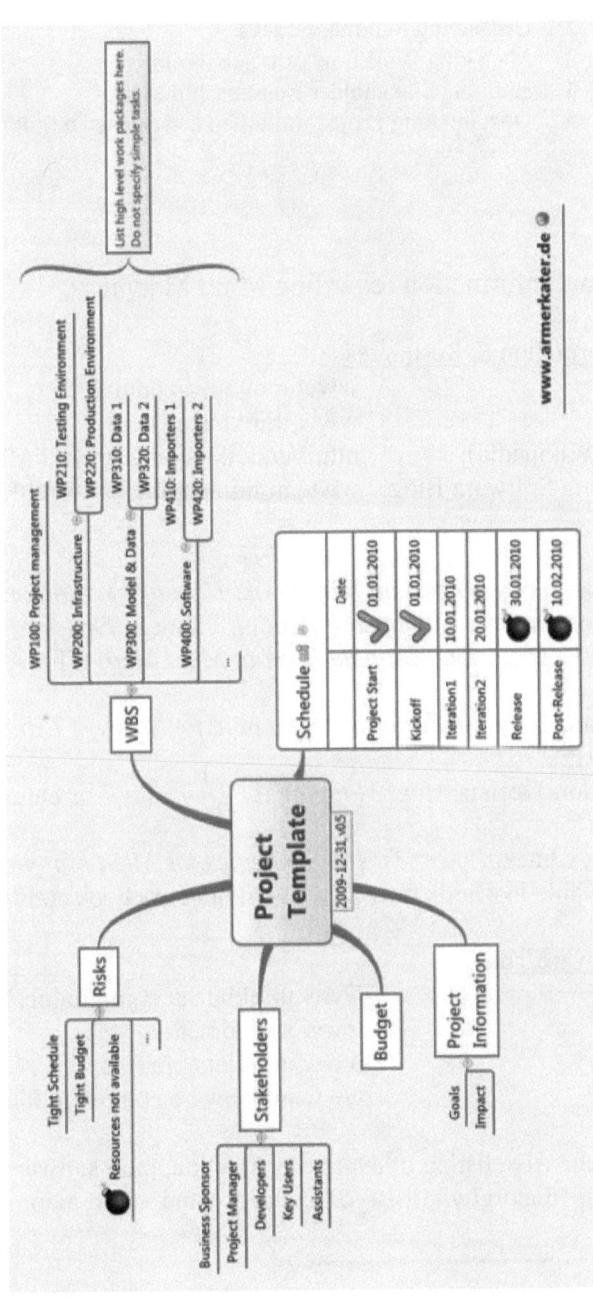

> ## Using Mind Maps in Project Management Practice:
>
> 1. Developing Work Breakdown Structures
> 2. Organizing Summary Tasks
> 3. Managing Workflow of a Sub-Team
> 4. Building Stakeholder Relationship Maps
> 5. Documenting Project Initiation and Scope Definition Sessions

For additional information regarding Mind Mapping[ii]:

General Information & Resources
Tony Buzan: www.tonybuzan.com
ThinkBuzan: www.thinkbuzan.com
Mind Map (Wikipedia):   http://en.wikipedia.org/wiki/Mind_map
Mind Mapping Software Blog: www.mindmappingsoftwareblog.com

Books
     Buzan, Tony, *The Mind Map Book: How to Use Radiant Thinking to Maximize Your Brain's Untapped Potential,* Plume, 1996
     Buzan, Tony, *The Ultimate Book of Mind Maps,* Thorsons Publishers, 2006
     Buzan, Tony, *Modern Mind Mapping for Smarter Thinking,* Proactive Thinking, 2012
     Rustler, Florian, *Mind Mapping for Dummies,* For Dummies Publishing, 2012
     Frey, Chuck, *Power Tips & Strategies for Mind Mapping Software, 3rd Edition,* available in eBook only at www.mindmap-ebook.com/v3/

Popular Software Tools
iMindMap™   www.thinkbuzan.com/products/imindmap/
XMind™   www.xmind.net
MindJet™   www.mindjet.com
MindView™   www.matchware.com/en/products/mindview

For a comprehensive listing of available mind mapping software tools:
http://en.wikipedia.org/wiki/List_of_concept-_and_mind-mapping_software

---

[ii] See Legal Disclaimer (pg. iv)

Process Mapping

Process mapping is a key tool that many organizations leverage to ensure business processes operate efficiently and effectively. In essence, a process map is simply a pictorial representation of the sequence of actions that comprise a process. Most utilized by business analysts, project managers and lean practitioners, mapping and charting of process activities is typically achieved through direct analysis and documentation of each step within a process.

Usage of process maps started in the manufacturing centers of the United States in the early 1920s as industrial engineers and motion study professionals began to seek out efficiency improvements in the industrial production process. The first structured method for documenting process flow, the flow process chart, was introduced by Frank Gilbreth to members of the American Society of Mechanical Engineers (ASME) in 1921 within the presentation titled, "Process Charts—First Steps in Finding the One Best Way".[17] This process gradually caught on in industrial engineering circles and eventually led to the business process mapping discipline known and in use today.

Ideally, the work involved in a particular business process follows the same steps every time and will involve only the necessary amount of resources and/or effort to complete. The primary goal of mapping business processes is to ensure that this is indeed true. Some secondary benefits of business process maps include:

- Serving as work flow training aids for new employees
- Continuous improvement (work simplification) initiatives

- Input into business resumption and disaster recovery planning
- Protection against loss of knowledge by key employee departures
- Automation of process steps

Successful process mapping starts with selecting the type of map/diagram to be used in order to visually depict the process. This documentation typically takes the form of a process flow (flow chart) diagram or a cross-functional process diagram (sometimes referred to as a "swim lane" diagram) if the process involves inputs or outputs to different business functions.

Once the map-type has been selected, the next step is to prepare and organize for the actual analysis and documentation. Much of the actual activity of mapping processes can be done via sticky notes, and there are several reasons to take that approach:

- They can represent a singular task or event in the process
- They can be easily moved around to represent the true, or desired, process as more and more steps are identified
- The tools needed are relatively inexpensive and readily available

Finally, adoption of a best practice method to physically perform the process mapping exercise will yield the most beneficial results.

The Four Major Steps of Process Mapping:[18]

1. Process Identification
   - Attaining a full understanding of all steps of a process
2. Information Gathering
   - Identifying objectives, risks, and key controls in a process
3. Interviewing and Mapping
   - Understanding the point of view of individuals in the process and designing actual maps
4. Analysis
   - Utilizing tools and approaches to make the process run more effectively and efficiently

Examples of process maps include:

Figure 4 - Basic Process Flow Chart

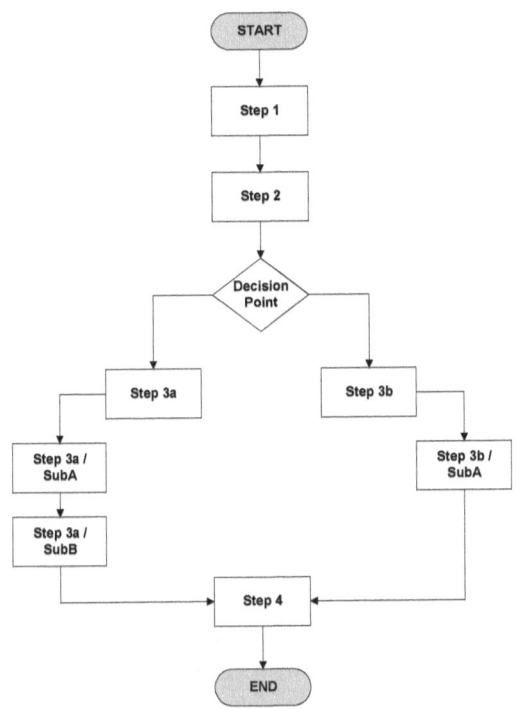

Figure 5 - Basic Cross-Functional (Swim lane) Flow Chart

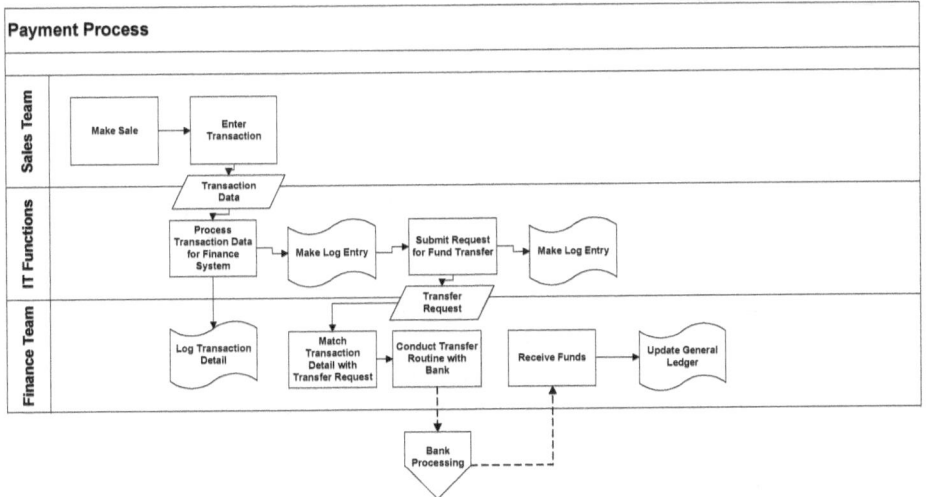

While the maps/charts depicted in the figures are quite simple, process maps in the "real-world" can become quite complex and detailed. Some maps simply document the steps in a process, while others detail work flow, timings, hand-offs, delays/wait times, business value vs. waste or even sub-process loops.

Using Process Maps in Project Management Practice:

1. Business Process Analysis
2. Lean Six Sigma Initiatives
3. Value Stream Mapping
4. Work Effort Estimation
5. Requirements Elicitation
6. Task Sequencing

For additional information regarding Process Mapping[iii]:

General Information & Resources

Process Mapping (Wikipedia):	wikipedia.org/wiki/Business_process_mapping
Process Excellence Network:	www.processExcellencenetwork.com
Orion Development Group:	www.odgroup.com/articles/map-process/

Books

Jacka, J. Mike & Keller, Paulette J, *Business Process Mapping: Improving Customer Satisfaction,* John Wiley & Sons, 2011

Damelio, Robert, *The Basics of Process Mapping,* Productivity Press, 2011

Madison, Dan, *Process Mapping, Process Improvement and Process Management*, Paton Press, 2005

Popular Software Tools

SmartDraw™	www.smartdraw.com
Microsoft Visio®	office.microsoft.com/Visio/
RFFlow™	www.rff.com
ProMap™	www.promapp.com
iGraphx™	www.igrapfx.com

[iii] See Legal Disclaimer (pg. iv)

Storyboarding

A storyboard is graphical organization of images or illustrations, displayed in sequence, to aid in visualizing flow, transition and overall scene "feel" of a media production. Storyboards bring focus to the scenes of the story being told and help to define any parameters the scene operates under, such as lighting, background, camera location, etc.

The concept of storyboarding was created by Walt Disney Productions in the early 1930s during the development of Snow White and the Seven Dwarfs to aid in the visualization and sequencing of scenes. In Christopher Finch's, *The Art of Walt Disney*[19], it is noted that Disney himself credited animator Webb Smith with creating the idea of drawing scenes on separate sheets of paper and pinning them up on a bulletin board to tell a story in sequence, thus creating the first storyboard.

While the vast majority of today's storyboard usage remains rooted in the entertainment industry, gradual adoption of the concept has filtered into other segments of the business world, including project management. Typical business usage of the storyboard revolves around presentation development such as corporate training, marketing campaigns or annual report documentation. In financial and accounting functions, usage can be found in the form of Activity Based Costing Systems. These systems develop a detailed and sequenced process flow, which visually shows all activities and the relationships among activities. They are used in this way to measure the cost of resources consumed, identify and eliminate non-value-added costs, determine the efficiency and effectiveness of all major activities, and identify and evaluate new activities that can improve future performance.[20] A more recent offshoot of the storyboarding concept has arisen within the Lean Six Sigma methodology in the form of a "Quality Storyboard." This method illustrates telling the story of the quality control process via individually ordered process steps that can be re-arranged in the search for the ideal flow or sequence alignment.

Storyboarding has experienced a resurgence of attention as of late from both mobile application developers and entrepreneurs seeking venture capital funding. Mobile application developers are using the tool to outline the flow, sequencing and transition of screens within "apps." It is also useful when considering options or changes to the software, as the proposed changes can easily be inserted anywhere in the process to get a feel for the flow of the user experience.

Entrepreneurs, on the other hand, have a need to develop short, but effective, "elevator speech" presentations to pitch to potential investors. They are finding the storyboarding tool to be effective in walking potential investors through a brief story of what their product/service is, how it's used, why someone would want it, etc.

The process of conducting a storyboarding session is quite simple. One of the first preparation tasks is to determine where to display the storyboard. Depending on the number of drawings/images, the space requirements may be quite large. A typical storyboard, however, can easily fit on one wall using sticky notes or scene template sheets.

Next, determine how the storyboard will be constructed. While sticky notes are fast and simple, scene template sheets provide consistency in how the scene is constructed. For example, Figure 6 depicts a blank storyboard scene template. This specific example provides for scene lead-in, the actual main scene and scene lead-out. This style helps integrate the transitions between larger scene concepts.

Figure 6 - Storyboard Scene Template

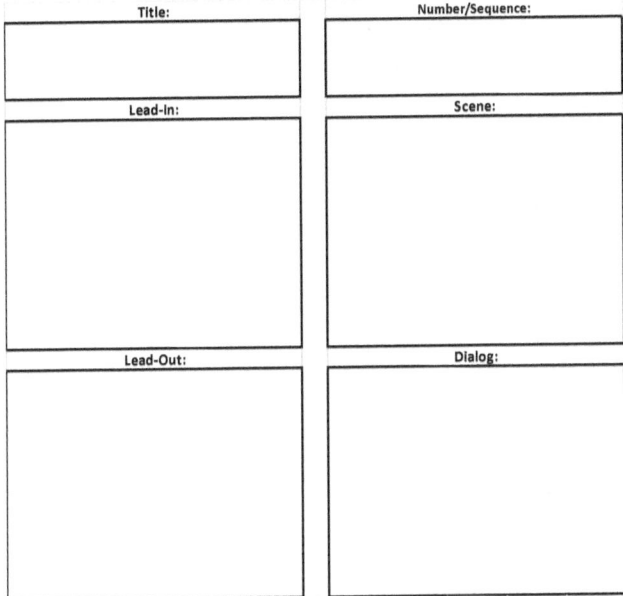

Figure 7 depicts a typical completed "scene card."

Figure 7 - Complete Scene Card

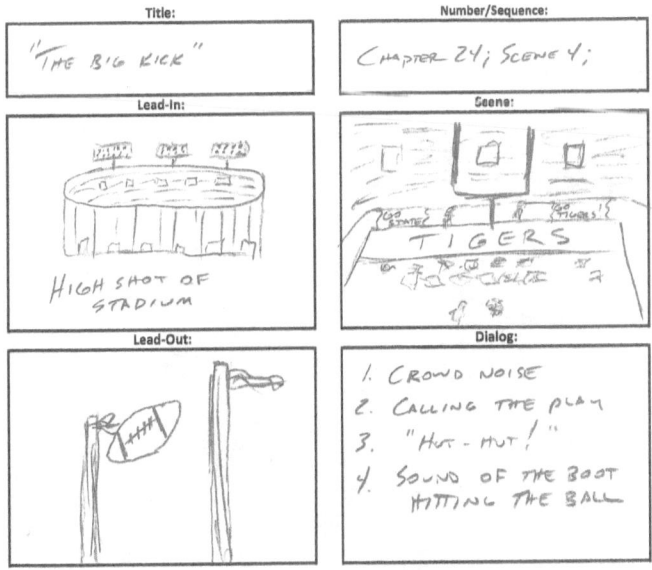

Figures 8 and 9 represent business examples of how storyboard cards are sequenced and displayed to represent the flow of the story or user experience.

Figure 8 - Card Sequence View

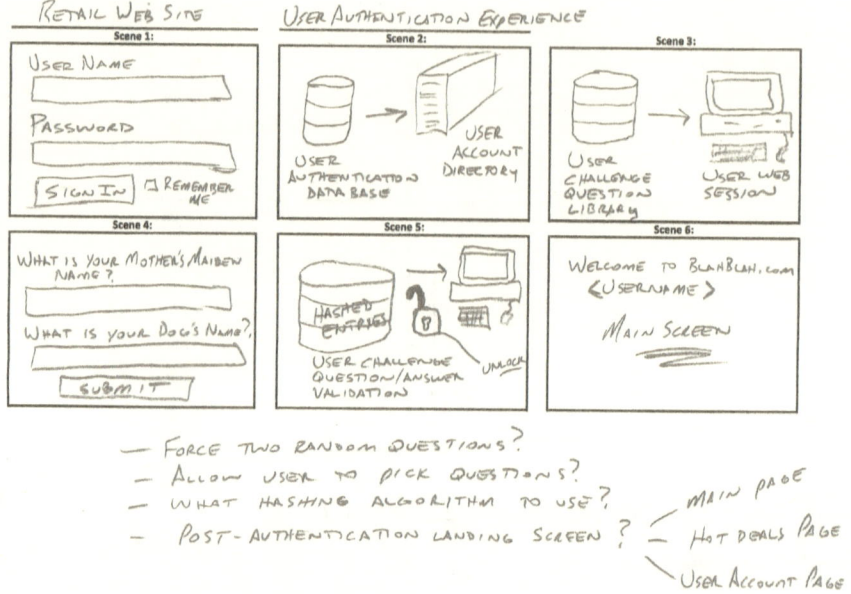

Figure 9 - Example Storyboard Wall

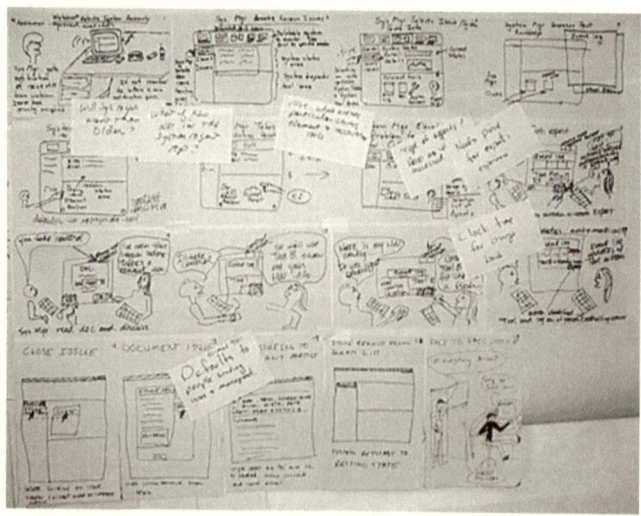

Storyboarding is a quick, informal way to organize information and shouldn't cause anxiety among those who consider themselves artistically challenged. Artistic ability is not required for effective storyboarding. Quick sketches and concepts are the rule here so keep it simple.

In project management discipline, storyboards are commonly used to communicate the phases and flow of work planned for a project effort. This is especially useful when communicating with project leadership and stakeholders as it allows them to have a key visual representation of the flow of work and, when used throughout the project, where the project's current state is in comparison to the overall "story" timeline.

When leveraged early in the project initiation and planning phases, storyboards are also an invaluable tool for defining the major deliverables and in what sequence they need to be performed. Because the storyboard is a depiction of the end-to-end process, it also becomes a great tool for conducting "what-if" scenarios, or for analyzing proposed changes, by moving certain processes or deliverables around in the overall flow of the effort to gauge impact or outcomes of potential changes.

> ## Using Storyboarding in Project Management Practice:
>
> 1. Task & Phase Sequencing
> 2. "What If" Scenario Planning
> 3. Change Impact Analysis
> 4. Timeline Creation/Planning
> 5. Resource Planning

For additional information regarding Storyboarding[iv]:

General Information & Resources

Storyboard (Wikipedia):	wikipedia.org/wiki/Storyboard
Univ. of Houston, Education:	tinyurl.com/lfobbwa (*case sensitive*)

Books

      Tumminello, Wendy, *Exploring Storyboarding,* Cengage Learning, 2004, ISBN 978-1-401-82715-1

      Jew, Anson, *Professional Storyboarding: Rules of Thumb,* Focal Press, 2013, ISBN 978-1-136-12673-4

      Rousseau, David and Phillips, Benjamin, *Storyboarding Essentials,* Watson-Guptill, 2013, ISBN 978-0-770-43694-0

Popular Software Tools

StoryboardThat ™	www.storyboardthat.com
Amazon Storyteller™	studios.amazon.com/storyteller
Storyboards3D ™	Apple® iOS App

[iv] See Legal Disclaimer (pg. iv)

Root Cause Analysis

It is an extremely rare occasion (if ever?) that projects get executed without encountering and resolving an issue of some kind. Because of this reality, problem solving tools such as root cause analysis are very valuable for project managers and their teams. When issues do arise, being able to quickly understand the root-level causation of the problem is critical for fixing the issue and getting the project back on track.

Root cause analysis is a method of problem solving that seeks to identify the base origin of a problem. A root cause is a cause that, once removed from the problem fault sequence, prevents the final undesirable event from recurring.[21] Root cause analysis became prevalent in the 1950s as a result of work being conducted by defense contractors for the National Aeronautics and Space Administration (NASA). Because even small systems failures within the fledgling space program would have potentially catastrophic results, increased focus was placed on identifying and correcting root causes of failures, rather than addressing only the symptoms as they appeared.

The concept and its usage accelerated rapidly in the 1960s and 1970s as lean manufacturing techniques were developed. Instead of focusing only on the symptoms of problems, resulting in the need to re-visit the fix of the problem over and over, the underlying systems and processes were scrutinized for causation. This elimination of "re-work" became the cornerstone of process improvement methodology still in use today.

In the search for the problem's origin, a process was developed to get to the root cause as quickly as possible, while still exploring all of the potential causes and inter-related effects and sub-causes.

Root cause analysis has three main steps in its process:

1. Define and Analyze the Problem
    a. What are the specific symptoms being observed?
    b. How do you know it's a "problem?"
    c. Is the problem repeatable?
2. Explore Cause, Effect and Impact
    a. What is the sequence of events that result in the problem?
    b. What are all of the potential causes of the problem and/or its symptoms?
3. Determine Root Cause and Remediate
    a. What is the actual causal factor of the problem?
    b. What is the corrective action and does it prevent the problem from recurring?
    c. After the fix has been implemented, has the corrective action been verified as a final resolution?

Root cause analysis has many visual-based tools and techniques to assist project management professionals with getting to the heart of problems that have the potential to stall projects. The most common of these tools is known as the "5 Whys" Approach, and it is a quick, but thought-provoking, exercise that frequently yields very positive results.

Sakichi Toyoda, an industrialist, the founder of Toyota Industries and often referred to as the "King of Japanese Inventors," developed the 5 Whys technique in the 1930s. 5 Whys is an iterative, question-asking technique used to explore the cause-and-effect relationships underlying a particular problem by drilling down through the symptoms to the ultimate underlying cause.

This "drill down" is accomplished by asking the question "why" to the first identified cause. When the answer to that cause is found, the question "why" is asked and answered again. This process is repeated no fewer than five times, thus the name 5 Whys.

The technique became popular in the lean manufacturing initiatives of 1970s and Toyota still uses it to solve problems today. It is also most effective when the answers come from people who have hands-on experience related to the process being examined.

Figure 10 - 5 Whys Technique

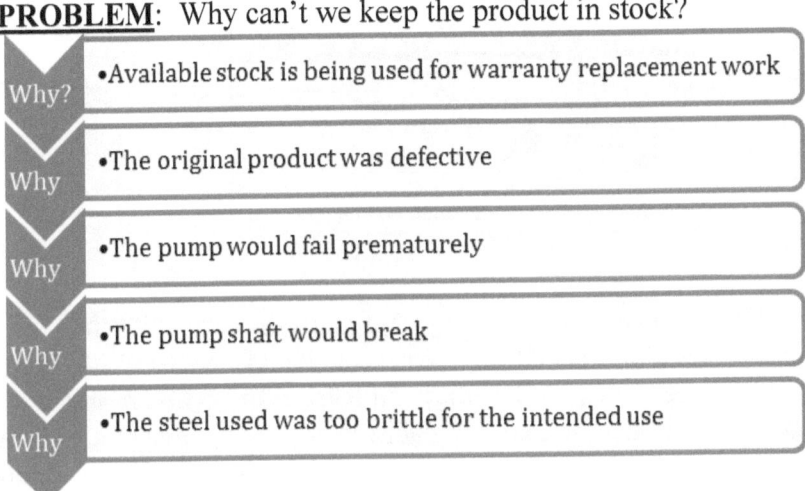

PROBLEM: Why can't we keep the product in stock?

Why? • Available stock is being used for warranty replacement work

Why • The original product was defective

Why • The pump would fail prematurely

Why • The pump shaft would break

Why • The steel used was too brittle for the intended use

Based on the example shown in Figure 10, some people might be tempted to just accept the first answer and move on. Those that remained would likely stop asking questions at the second result. But unless a person knew that the steel used for the pump shaft was too brittle for the designed use, the problem would keep recurring. In other words, the root cause would not have been found. Does it always take exactly five rounds every time? No, sometimes the root cause is found in as early as three rounds or as many as ten, but the vast majority come within the first five iterations.

The second most utilized root cause analysis tool is the "Ishikawa (Fishbone)" Diagram. Also known as cause-and-effect analysis, the method was devised by Professor Kaoru Ishikawa, a pioneer of quality management at Kawasaki Shipyards in the 1960s. The diagrams created with the tool are known as fishbone diagrams because a completed diagram can look like the skeleton of a fish. (see Figure 11)

Figure 11 - Ishikawa (Fishbone) Diagram

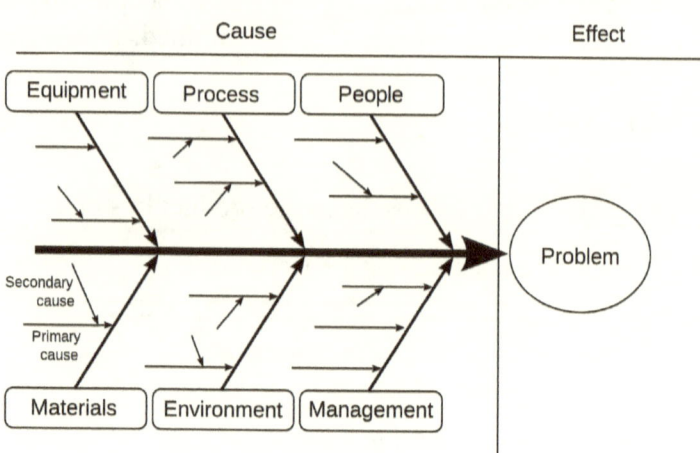

The exercise of cause and effect analysis starts with the definition of the problem on the right. Working backward from the problem statement, effects (symptoms) that result from the problem are assessed. A cause is then determined for each effect, being aware that primary causes can also have secondary causes. While there are many industry-specific templates[22] of this tool available, the most common include summary-level factors commonly seen in the manufacturing world such as: People, Process, Equipment, Materials, Environment and Management. They serve as "food for thought" in uncovering potential causes to the problem.

Finally, the practice of "Failure Mode and Effects Analysis" or FMEA, has been shown to be extremely effective in conducting system failure analysis and estimating the potential likelihood and impact of a failure. Developed by reliability engineers in the 1950s to study problems that might arise from malfunctions of military systems, FMEA involves reviewing as many components, assemblies, and subsystems as possible to identify real or potential failure modes, including their causes and effects. For each component, the failure modes and their resulting effects on the rest of the system are recorded in a specific FMEA worksheet.[23] (see Figure 12)

Figure 12 - Failure Mode & Effect Analysis

Reference ID	Item Description	Potential Failure Mode	Potential Failure Cause
1.1.1	Oxygen Supply Valve to Main Combustion Unit A	Valve May Fail to Close	Failure to Lubricate Valve

Immediate Effect of Failure	Secondary Effect of Failure	Probability	Severity
Failure to Reduce or Stop Flow of Oxygen to Main Combustion Unit A	Main Combustion Unit A Failure	Remote	Catastrophic

Detection Method	Risk Level (P*S)+D	Actions Needed	Mitigation Plan
Valve Position Indicator on Panel D, Indicator Gauge 312	Unacceptable	Valve Lubrication Verification on Pre-Flight Checklist	Add Item to Pre-Flight Checklist

Walking through this exercise at a component by component level can help to identify potential failure modes based on experience with similar products and processes. The FMEA is essentially a forward logic analysis, however the failure probability can only be estimated or reduced by understanding the failure mechanism. Ideally this probability should be lowered to "impossible to occur" by defining and eliminating the root cause(s).

Because the vast majority of root cause analysis tools in use across industry today stem from the Quality, Lean and/or Six Sigma methodologies, it is recommended that additional information on this topic be sought directly from organizations that specialize in those fields such as:

- American Society for Quality
- Toyota Production System
- Total Quality Management

Using Root Cause Analysis in Project Management Practice:

1. Issue Management / Problem Solving
2. Risk Management
3. Lessons Learned
4. Project Quality Management

For additional information regarding Root Cause Analysis[v]:

General Information & Resources

Root Cause Analysis (Wikipedia):	wikipedia.org/wiki/root_cause_analysis
American Society for Quality (ASQ):	www.asq.org

Books

Andersen, Bjorn and Fagerhaug, Tom, *The ASQ Pocket Guide to Root Cause Analysis,* ASQ Quality Press, 2013, ISBN 978-0-873-89863-8

Okes, Duke, *Root Cause Analysis: The Core of Problem Solving and Corrective Action,* ASQ Quality Press, 2009, ISBN 978-0-873-89764-8

ABS Consulting (multiple authors), *Root Cause Analysis Handbook,* Rothstein Associates, 2008, ISBN 978-1-931-33251-4

Carlson, Carl, *Effective FMEAs,* Wiley, 2012, ISBN 978-1-118-00743-3

Popular Software Tools

Microsoft Excel®	office.microsoft.com/Excel®
Reason™	www.rootcause.com
CauseLink™	www.sologic.com/root-cause-analysis-software

[v] See Legal Disclaimer (pg. iv)

Charting, Diagramming & Graphing

The bulk of all data visualization takes the form of a simple chart, diagram or graph. In use across all varieties of business enterprise, a chart is simply is a graphical representation of data, in which "the data is represented by symbols, such as bars in a bar chart, lines in a line chart, or slices in a pie chart".[24]   Charts ease understanding of data and demonstrate various interrelationships that occur between data sets. Charts are typically read and understood more quickly than simple raw, numerical data since the human brain is generally able to infer meaning from pictures much quicker than from text or numbers alone.

The nomenclature used for a chart is typically interchangeable with the terms 'diagram' or 'graph.' Regardless, they all refer to a diagrammatical illustration of a set of data. They are most often created by hand (sketch) or by computer using a charting application like Microsoft Excel®.

Rather than attempting to draw distinctions between a chart, diagram or graph, it is more valuable to understand which types of charts are more useful for presenting a given data set over another. For example, data that is represented in percentages (fractional share, preference or departmental) is often displayed in a pie chart. Comparing the sum totals of particular sets of data (number of instances), on the other hand, may be more easily understood when presented in a vertical bar chart. Or, data representing numbers that change over a period of time (revenue, expenses or staffing) might be best shown as a line chart.

Charts share a number of similar features that make it easier to understand what the data represents and serve as a frame of reference for viewer:

Axis:
- Bar, line and other similar charts often display data on a field of axes. Horizontal (x) and vertical (y) axis frame the field in which the data is analyzed. On some occasions where the data is presented in 3D format, the depth (z) axis is added.

Scale:
- Each axis must have a scale. Scale provides the ratio of the size of a model or other representation to the actual size of the object represented. Scale is frequently sub-divided by periodic graduation marks to aid the viewer in spatial reference.

Label:
- Each axis will typically also have a label displayed outside or beside it, briefly describing the dimension represented.

Grid:
- Within the graph, a grid of lines may appear to aid in the visual alignment of data. Using the appropriate scale, major and minor grid lines can be set, with major grid lines typically being enhanced or emphasized to define the intervals.

Data Points
- The data of a chart can be represented in any number of formats. For example, data may appear as dots, lines, symbols or shapes. The individual data points can be connected or unconnected, or they can take on any combination of colors and patterns.

Legend or Key
- When the data appearing in a chart contains multiple variables, the chart may include a legend (also known as a key). A legend contains a list of the variables appearing in the chart and an example of their appearance. This information allows the data from each variable to be identified in the chart.

Common Types of General Charts, Diagrams & Graphs:

Figure 13 - Example of a Bar Chart

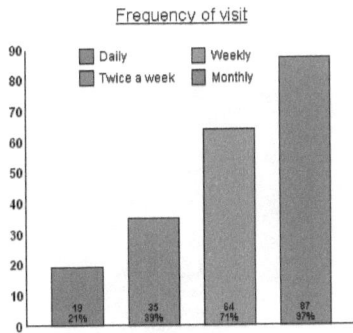

Bar Chart: A chart with rectangular bars having lengths proportional to the values that they represent. The bars can be plotted vertically or horizontally. A vertical bar chart is sometimes called a column bar chart.

Figure 14 - Example of a Line Chart

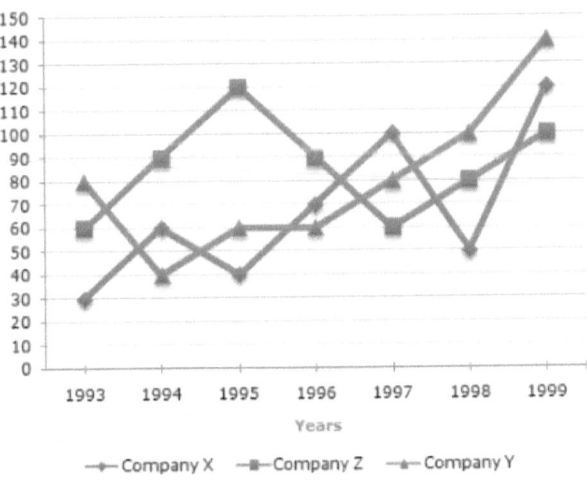

Line Chart: A type of chart which displays information as a series of data points called 'markers' which are connected by straight line segments. Information is most typically presented as a time series with the x-axis moving chronologically from left to right. Earned value calculations on projects take the visual form of a line chart.

Figure 15 - Example of a Pie Chart

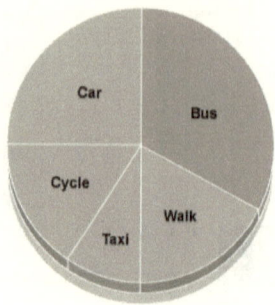

Pie Chart: A circular statistical graphic, which is divided into sectors to illustrate numerical proportion, or percentage of the whole. In project management, this is used frequently to display the breakdown of different resource or cost types.

Figure 16 - Example of a Radar Chart

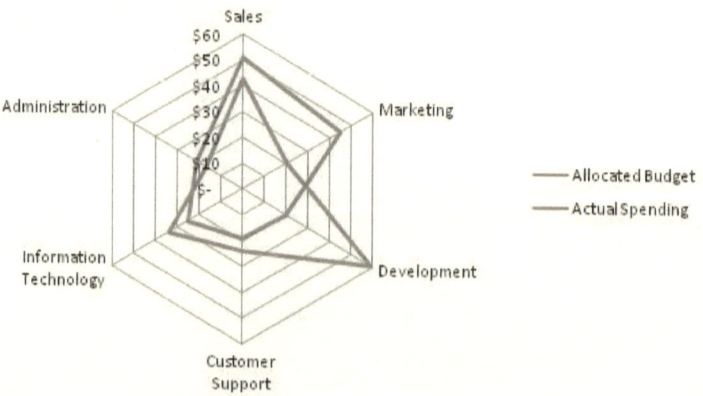

Radar Chart: A graphical method of displaying data for two or more variables in the form of a two-dimensional chart of three or more quantitative variables represented on axes starting from the same point. (also known as a Spider, Web or Star Chart). Radar charts are popular for showing pre- and post-event changes, such as process improvement measurements.

Figure 17 - Example of a Bubble Chart

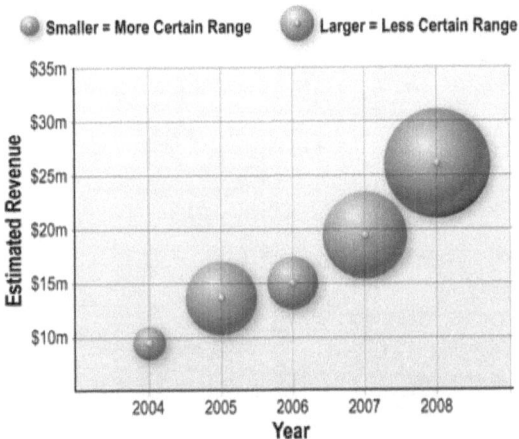

Bubble Chart: A type of chart that displays three dimensions of data. Bubble charts are frequently used to facilitate the understanding of social, economic, medical, and other scientific relationships. In project management discipline, it is very commonly used as a way to map out project portfolio investment balance and is typically presented to show strategic alignment (x-axis), impact (y-axis) and size of effort (data point size).

Figure 18 - Example of a Waterfall Chart

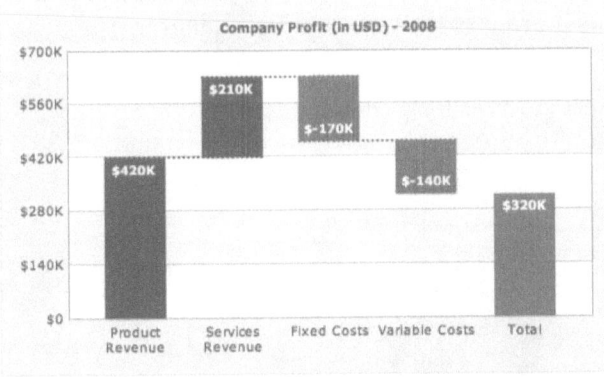

Waterfall Chart: A type of chart used to depict the cumulative effect of sequentially introduced positive or negative values. Demonstrates how an initial value is affected by a series of intermediate positive or negative value-based events.   For project management applications, waterfall charts are used to show costs versus expected payback.

Figure 19 - Example of a Flow Chart

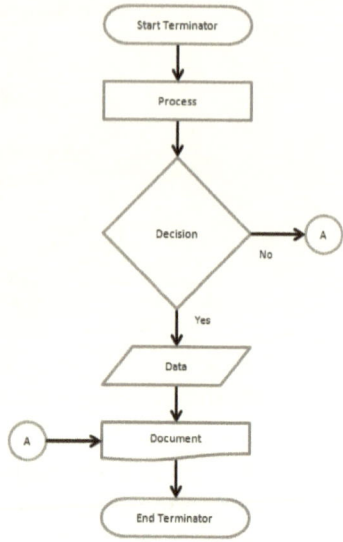

Flow Chart: A type of diagram that represents a workflow or process, showing the steps as boxes of various kinds, and their order, by connecting them with directional (flow) arrows. Generic guidelines on consistent usage of the symbols and graphics used do exist. Industry-specific standards are also applicable to their individual areas of interest. (also known as a process flow or data flow diagram)

Figure 20 - Example of a Venn Diagram

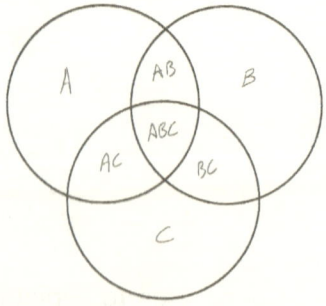

Venn Diagram: A diagram that shows all possible logical relations (overlap) between a finite collection of different data sets.

Figure 21 - Example of a Histogram

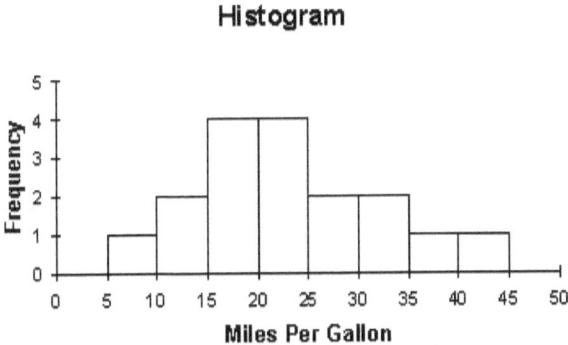

Histogram: A graphical representation of the distribution of data by showing the proportion of cases that fall into one of each of several defined categories and providing a sense of data density. Histograms that sort the x-axis values in descending order from left-to-right are known as Pareto Charts and are very useful in root cause analysis to show the most common source of defects so they can be remediated with the hope of drastically reducing their number and frequency.

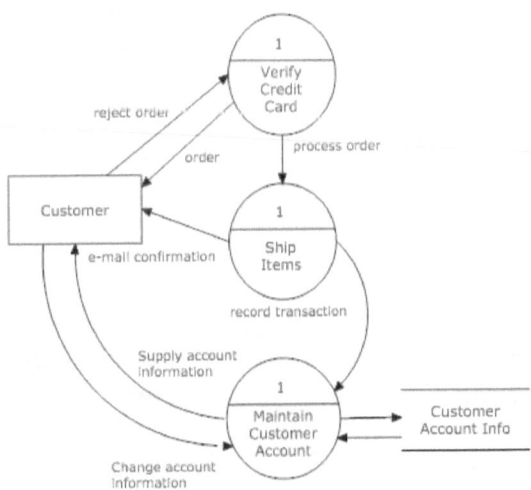

Data Flow Diagram: A graphical representation of the "flow" of data through an information system. Often used in software development projects to simplify otherwise complex back-end processes.

Common Types of Project Management Charts, Diagrams & Graphs:

Figure 22 - Example of a Gantt Chart

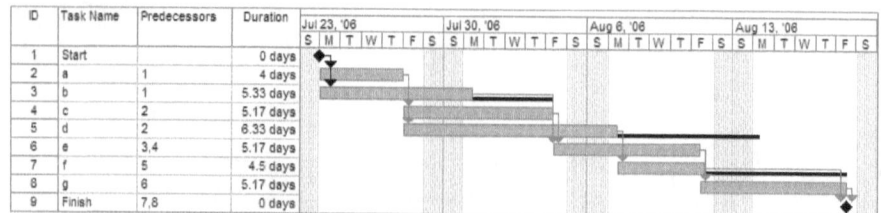

ID	Task Name	Predecessors	Duration
1	Start		0 days
2	a	1	4 days
3	b	1	5.33 days
4	c	2	5.17 days
5	d	2	6.33 days
6	e	3,4	5.17 days
7	f	5	4.5 days
8	g	6	5.17 days
9	Finish	7,8	0 days

Gantt Chart: A type of bar chart, developed by Henry Gantt in the 1910s, that illustrates a project schedule.[25] [26] [27] Summary task, task level and milestone elements of the work breakdown structure of the project comprise what is typically represented on the Gantt chart. Gantt charts can also show dependency (i.e., precedence network) relationships between activities and tasks, as well as depicting current schedule status by using percent-complete shadings and a vertical marker line to represent the current date.

Figure 23 - Example of a Project Network Diagram / PERT Chart

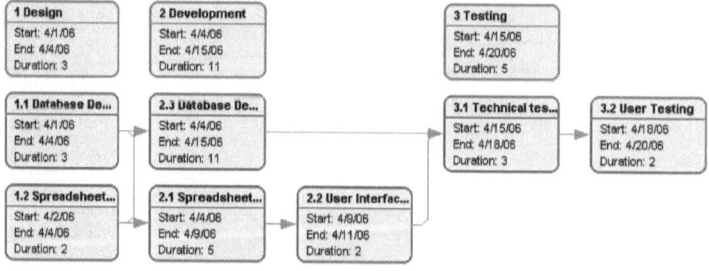

Project Network Diagram (PERT Charting): A graphical flow chart that depicts the sequence of a project's detailed task-level elements, including all pertinent dependencies. The project network diagram is drawn from left to right to reflect project chronology. Modern day project network diagramming is a derivation of a more complex, but similar, past technique known as 'PERT.'

PERT is the acronym for Program Evaluation and Review Technique, which is a method of analyzing all of the tasks involved in completing a given project, especially the time needed to complete each task, in order to identify the minimum time needed to complete the total project, also known as the 'critical path.' Developed primarily to simplify the planning and scheduling of large, complex and interdependent projects, it was developed for the U.S. Navy Special Projects Office in 1957 to support the U.S. Navy's Polaris nuclear submarine project.[28]

Using Charting Tools in Project Management Practice:

1. Project Scheduling
2. Process Diagramming
3. Status Reporting
4. Statistical Analysis

For additional information regarding Charting Tools[vi]:

General Information & Resources

Charting (Wikipedia):	en.wikipedia.org/wiki/Chart
Visual Literacy Project:	bit.ly/IX1bvI *(case sensitive)*
OpenLearn Works:	www.open.edu (search diagrams, charts and graphs)
VizThink:	www.vizthink.com
Visual Management Blog:	www.xqa.com.ar/visualmanagement/

Books

     Yau, Nathan, *Visualize This: The FlowingData Guide to Design, Visualization and Statistics,* Wiley, 2011, ISBN 978-0-470-94488-2

     Few, Stephen, *Show Me The Numbers: Designing Tables and Graphs to Enlighten,* Analytics Press, 2012, ISBN 978-0-970-60197-1

     Tufte, Edward, *The Visual Display of Quantitative Information, Graphics Press,* 2001, ISBN 978-0-961-39214-7

Popular Software Tools

Microsoft OfficeSuite®	office.microsoft.com
Google Docs®	docs.google.com
ChartGo™	www.chartgo.com
MakeChart™	www.makechart.com
Online Chart Tool™	www.onlinecharttool.com

For a comprehensive listing of popular charting and diagramming tools, please see the Visual Thinking Elements Gallery developed by Adam Sicinski at: www.VisualThinkingMagic.com

---

[vi] See Legal Disclaimer (pg. iv)

<u>Notes</u>

Drawing / Sketching

Drawing out concepts or thoughts is one of the simplest and most efficient means of communicating visual ideas. Using quick hand drawn scenes or sketching out a product design can quickly bring clarity to complex issues and provide insight into confusing concepts. Drawings are many times a "spur-of-the-moment" capture of "what if…" thoughts or ideas. This makes them exploratory in nature, with considerable emphasis on direct observation, problem-solving and current context.

There are many different methods of drawing that are formally recognized. This book however, will only focus on two, sketching and doodling. Sketches are quick, unrefined drawings used to record or develop ideas for later use. Because they are not intended to accurately depict a final working idea, it is a quick way of graphically demonstrating an image, idea, concept or principle. Somewhat similar, doodles are rudimentary drawings at an even more abstract level. Typically taking the form of shapes or concepts, doodling helps to organize thoughts, aid in memory recall and stimulate create problem solving.

One of the biggest hang ups people have with sketching or doodling is the thought, "I can't draw!" Quite frankly, artistic ability has very little to do with effective sketching. In some cases, having a detailed artistic eye can even be a hindrance! The whole point of a sketch is not how well a person can draw, but what kind of information they are trying to convey. A sketch is simply a representation of the "visual" image that a person has in their mind.

Despite all of the idea management and organizational software, mobile applications and cloud-based product suites available in the marketplace today, drawing is still the easiest and fastest way to facilitate discussions that spark a wide variety of ideas and examine alternative options. Sketch-based collaboration is also frequently a group effort. It is not uncommon to see one person in the group start a drawing of an idea and then have two or three others either build off of the original drawing or add their own idea to the sheet.

One of the more recent trends promoting sketching and doodling in the workplace is the concept of napkin-based drawing made popular by Dan Roam in his book, *"The Back of the Napkin."*[29] The basic premise in his book is simple, that any problem can be solved with a simple picture drafted on nothing more complicated than a cocktail napkin. By drawing out the various components of a problem, the "back of the napkin" sketch becomes the spark that leads to productive creative problem solving.

While perhaps based more in myth than reality, take the story of how Southwest Airlines was conceived with a simple napkin drawing. Founders Herb Kelleher and Rollin King figured out how to beat the traditional hub-and-spoke airlines using a bar napkin and a pen. The two men drew three dots to represent Dallas, Houston, and San Antonio. Then, using arrows to represent direct flights between the cities, the idea was born for a low-cost, ultra-efficient airline.

Similarly, a hand-written drawing exists in the Walt Disney Company Archives, purportedly drawn by Walt Disney himself on a restaurant napkin during one of his site visits to the central Florida area, of a rough layout for EPCOT® and the Disney World Project in Florida. Remarkably, the actual layout of today's Walt Disney World® property bears a striking resemblance to this original sketch-based concept.

Of all the varied visual project management methods, drawing is one of the easiest and cheapest to undertake. Here are some ideas on how to get started using sketches and doodles in the workplace and among project teams:

1. Paper
    a. While this may seem self-explanatory, it is actually a good idea to utilize a number of different kinds of paper: blank, lined, graph, butcher, multi-colored construction, easel pad, etc.

b. Encourage project team members to carry and use a sketch pad or project journal to capture ideas and drawings when inspiration hits

2. Writing Instruments
    a. Again, aim a bit higher than the plain old No. 2 pencil or ballpoint pen. Try using colored pencils, markers, crayons, highlighters, fancy pens, etc.

3. Drawing Tools
    a. Drawing guides/templates, shape stencils or drafting tools like a compass, protractor or triangle

4. Group Drawing Tools
    a. Sticky notes, white boards, conference room wall with erasable marker paint finish, "old school" chalkboards, easels with pads, etc.

5. Electronic
    a. Smartphones, Tablets, electronic note taking or sketch pad capture devices, etc.

Drawing is perhaps most commonly used in project scoping sessions where the project's overall look and feel is still under development. But, when issues arise or risks are triggered on projects, don't overlook the value that sketches or doodles can provide in problem solving and alternative solution development.

Figure 24 - Sample Sketch – Buyer Purchase Experience

Figure 25 - Sample Doodle – Strategic Horizon

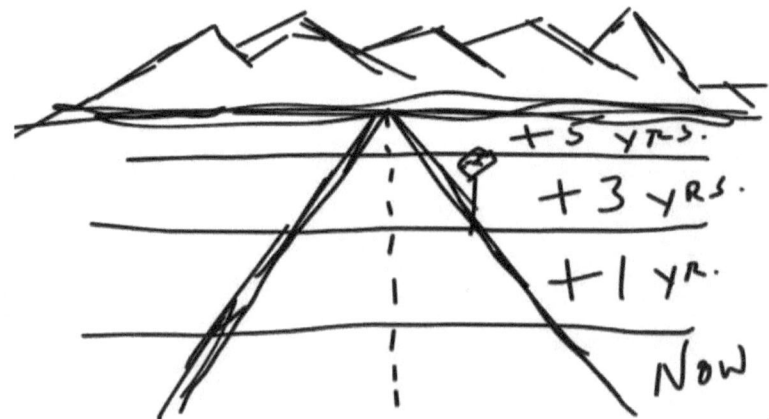

Using Drawing Concepts in Project Management Practice:

1. Project Scoping
2. Project Workflow Planning
3. Process Mapping
4. Creative Problem Solving
5. Strategic Planning & Visioning

For additional information regarding Drawing / Sketching concepts[vii]:

General Information & Resources
Sketching (Wikipedia):   en.wikipedia.org/wiki/Sketch_(drawing)
Doodle (Wikipedia):   en.wikipedia.org/wiki/Doodle
Sketching At Work: www.sketchingatwork.com/index.php/en/

Books
    Roam, Dan, *The Back of the Napkin,* Penguin Group, 2009, ISBN 978-1-591-84269-9
    Roam, Dan, *Unfolding the Napkin,* Penguin Group, 2009, ISBN 978-1-591-84319-1
    Brown, Sunni, *The Doodle Revolution: Unlock the Power to Think Differently,* Portfolio Hardcover, 2014, ISBN 978-1-591-84588-1
    Rohde, Mike, *The Sketchnote Handbook: The Illustrated Guide to Visual Note-Taking,* Peachpit Press, 2012, ISBN 978-0-321-85789-7

Popular Software Tools
SketchPro™   www.autodesk.com/products/sketchbook-pro/
Sketch Rolls™   www.sketchrolls.com/
SketchPad™   www.sketchi.io/sketchpad

[vii] See Legal Disclaimer (pg. iv)

Notes

Wireframes & Use Cases

Wireframes are traditionally the domain of marketing and web development professionals. Also known as a mock-up, screen sketch or page drawing, a wireframe is a visual representation of the framework of a presentation, document artifact or website. Wireframes make arranging and rearranging specific design elements easier when considering layouts and design esthetics. On some wireframes, transitions from one page or concept to another are also depicted. Other common additions to wireframes include interfaces with technology, webpage navigation methods and common frame components (page menu, photo/graphic, text box, menu, etc.)

Wireframes are commonly generated using either software applications or drawings/sketches and are generally created by business analysts, user experience (UX) designers, web developers, web designers and other roles with expertise in process management and information architecture. Developers use wireframes to get a more tangible grasp of the site's functionality and specific coding needs, while designers use them to depict the look, feel and branding. Where business analysts might use wireframes to visually identify business process flow or integration of business rules, user experience designers and information architects might use wireframes to show specific navigation paths between pages and back office components. Finally, project stakeholders and team members review wireframes to ensure that requirements and objectives are met through the design.

Figure 26 - Webpage Wireframe Drawing Example

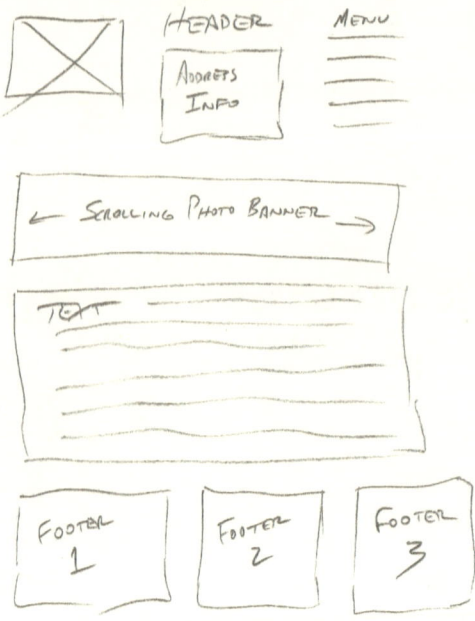

Use Cases are a bit different than wireframes but convey similar information. A use case is essentially the flow, or list of steps, that define the interactions between screens, steps in a process or other flow within a system.

The majority of the time, use cases are written from the user's perspective. It outlines, from a user's point of view, a system's behavior as it responds to a request. Each use case is represented as a sequence of simple steps, beginning with a user's goal and ending when that goal is fulfilled.

In 1986, Ivar Jacobson first formulated textual, structural, and visual modeling techniques for specifying use cases. Then in 1992, his co-authored book *Object-Oriented Software Engineering - A Use Case Driven Approach[30]*, helped to popularize the technique of capturing functional business requirements for conversion into technical requirements, especially in software development projects.

Use cases add value because they help explain how the system should behave. Similarly, because the entire process is mapped out, use cases also help brainstorm what could potentially go wrong. They also provide a list of goals, results, interactions and other data points. These data points can then be used to establish the cost, effort and complexity of the overall system. During project scoping meetings, the project team can then negotiate which functions become formal requirements and are included within the project.

Figure 27 – Use Case Example

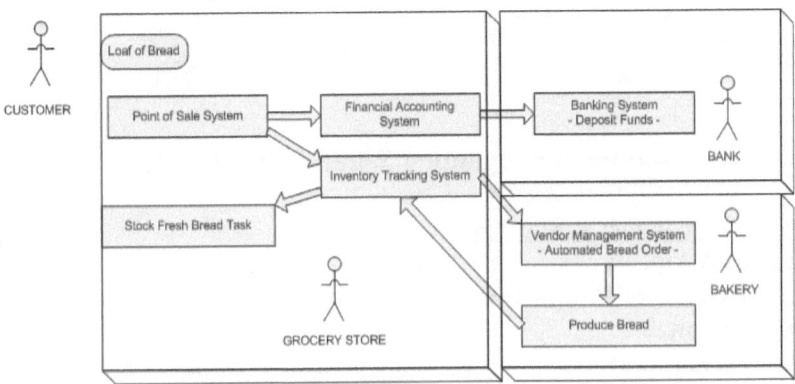

Use cases make it clear what a system is going to do and, by intentional omission, what it is not going to do. Wireframes on the other hand, make it clear what the user experience is going to look like and how the user will move through the system and/or process. They enable effective scope management, promote communication among project team members, and help bring visibility and clarity to business processes. In essence, wireframes and use cases ensure that the system being developed meets the business requirements of the system as it was envisioned.

Using Wireframes & Use Case Concepts in Project Management Practice:

1. Project Scoping
2. Functional Business Requirements
3. Technical Requirements Design & Development
4. Business Process Analysis

For additional information regarding Wireframe & Use Case concepts[viii]:

General Information & Resources
Wireframe (Wikipedia):   en.wikipedia.org/wiki/Website_wireframe
Beginner's Guide to Wireframing: bit.ly/1spBk2k (*case sensitive*)
Wireframe Showcase: www.wireframeshowcase.com
Use Case (Wikipedia):   en.wikipedia.org/wiki/Use_case
Ivar Jacobson International (Use Cases): www.ivarjacobson.com

Books
       Hamm, Matthew, *Wireframing Essentials*, Packt Publishing, 2014,
ISBN 978-1-849-69854-2
       Unger, Russ and Chandler, Carolyn, *A Project Guide to UX Design*,
New Riders, 2012, ISBN 978-0-321-81538-5
       Cockburn, Alistair, *Writing Effective Use Cases*, Addison-Wesley,
2000, ISBN 978-0-201-70225-5
       Jacobson, Ivar, *Object Oriented Software Engineering: A Use Case
Driven Approach*, Addison-Wesley, 1992, ISBN 978-0-201-54435-0

Popular Software Tools
Mockingbird Wireframing™   www.gomockingbird.com
Wireify ™   www.wirify.com
Case Complete™   www.casecomplete.com
Visual Use Case™   www.visualusecase.com
Creately™   www.creately.com/diagram-type/use-case

[viii] See Legal Disclaimer (pg. iv)

Visual Project Reporting

Earned Value Analysis

Earned Value Analysis (General)

Earned Value Analysis, as defined within the Project Management Institute's *Project Management Body of Knowledge* (PMBoK), is "the methodology that combines scope, schedule and resource measurements to assess project performance."[31] Put more simply, it is a technique for reporting project performance using quantitative data. The data may be presented in numerical (formulaic) or graphical (visual) format. Additionally, earned value analysis continuously measures project progress throughout the planned life cycle of the project, provides forecasts for likely project completion and can identify potential problems in schedule and/or budgetary performance early enough to take corrective action. While the application of earned value performance management was traditionally reserved for larger, more complex project efforts due to the increased level of rigor required to acquire and track performance data points, even small initiatives can benefit from the technique.

Earned Value Analysis or Management (EVA/EVM), like so many other project management tools, was developed in the 1960s as a financial analysis method for large governmental and industrial manufacturing programs. It takes its origins from the Program Evaluation and Review Technique (PERT), referenced earlier in this work, and its later counterpart the Cost/Schedule Control Systems Criteria (C/SCSC) approach used by the United States Department of

Defense.[32]　　While these two approaches eventually fell out of favor as being too burdensome and not applicable to all project types, the desire to measure cost, schedule and scope based metrics, and the interplay of those metrics, remained active among project management professionals.

As the use of EVM expanded within the U.S. Federal Government, its ever increasing exposure and adoption led to its eventual "codification" as *American National Standards Institute/Electronic Industry Alliance's (ANSI/EIA) 748-A Standard for EVMS*. Finally, EVM's inclusion within the first *Guide to the Project Management Body of Knowledge®*, published by the Project Management Institute in 1987, ensured its place as a favored project reporting tool.

At its most basic level, EVM involves four distinct steps:

1. Defining all of the work to be completed as part of the project at a task or activity level
   a. Developing a Work Breakdown Structure (WBS), or hierarchy of tasks, summary tasks and/or deliverables
2. Defining the Planned Value (PV) for each of the tasks or activities identified in step 1
   a. The cumulative planned value of all tasks on a project is also known as the Budget At Completion (BAC)
3. Defining how the work, at the task or activity level, will be considered "finished" for the purposes of depicting Earned Value (EV), also referred to as the percent complete or the accumulated "value" of completed tasks.
   a. 0/100 Rule: The task must be fully completed to be counted as "earned"
   b. 50/50 Rule: The task is shown as 50% complete when started and earns the remaining 50% of value when fully completed
   c. 25/75 Rule: A variation of the 50/50 Rule to encourage more focus on completion rather than simply starting work on tasks
4. Execution of the project task plan and recording actual costs, effort, duration and completion of the tasks that make up the plan.

Using this information, Earned Value becomes a project performance measurement in "real time" through the plotting of the aforementioned value metrics on a grid to visually display actual status vs. the planned baseline.

1. Planned Value (PV)
   a. How much work was estimated or planned to be completed by the current date in the project (and beyond)
2. Actual Cost (AC)
   a. The actual cost of work performed up to the current date of the project
3. Earned Value (EV)
   a. How much actual value has been delivered through the completion of work up to the current date of the project

Figure 28 - Simple Earned Value Chart Example

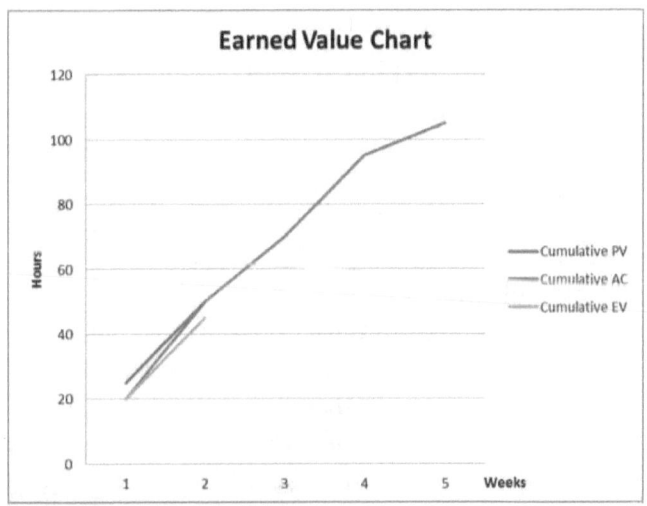

Metrics (in hours)	Week				
	1	2	3	4	5
Planned Value of Tasks (PV)	20	30	20	25	10
Actual Cost of Effort (AC)	25	25			
Earned Value of Tasks Completed (EV)	20	25			

* Most Recently Completed Week: Week 2

Metrics (in hours)	Week				
	1	2	3	4	5
Cumulative PV	20	50	70	95	105
Cumulative AC	25	50			
Cumulative EV	20	45			

As depicted in Figure 28, the planned value of the entire project effort is represented by the longest line. This is the "baseline" of how the project should proceed as per the defined plan. Deviations from this baseline reflect potential or actual issues from planned progress. In the figure, the shorter line above the planned value represents actual cost. This line shows that the project incurred higher actual costs as the project started, but has since moved back in line with the plan. Conversely, the shorter line underneath the planned value seen in the diagram represents earned value. This line shows that earned value originally tracked with the plan, but has since fallen behind schedule on delivering the expected value.

Going beyond simple recording and mapping of these baseline metrics, additional calculations can be leveraged to obtain a better understanding of project performance.   These include variance calculations and performance indices:

1. Variance Calculations:
    a. Cost Variance (CV) = EV − AC
        i. A CV of zero would mean the project is tracking exactly to budget, while a negative number would represent an <u>over</u> budget condition and a number greater than zero would represent an <u>under</u> budget condition
        ii. Using the data in Figure 28, the cost variance would be: CV= -5, (45 − 50) or over budget
    b. Schedule Variance (SV) = EV − PV
        i. An SV of zero would mean the project is tracking exactly on schedule, while a number greater than zero would represent the project as <u>ahead</u> of schedule and a negative number would represent the project as <u>behind</u> schedule.
        ii. Using the data in Figure 28, the schedule variance would be: SV= -5, (45-50) or reflective of a project that is behind schedule
2. Performance Indices:
    a. Cost Performance Index $(CPI) = \frac{EV}{AC}$
        i. CPI indicators break-down as follows:
            • < 1 means that the cost of completing the work is <u>higher than planned</u>

- - = 1 means that the cost of completing the work is right on plan
  - > 1 means that the cost of completing the work is <u>less than planned</u>
  ii. Using the data in Figure 28, the cost performance index would be: CPI = 0.9, $(\frac{45}{50})$ or a project that is completing work at a lower cost than originally planned
 b. Schedule Performance Index $(SPI) = \frac{EV}{PV}$
  i. SPI indicators break-down as follows:
   - < 1 means that the work is taking <u>longer than planned</u> to complete
   - = 1 means that the work is getting completed exactly as planned
   - > 1 means that the work is taking <u>less time than planned</u> to complete
  iii. Using the data in Figure 28, the cost performance index would be: SPI = 0.9, $(\frac{45}{50})$ or a project that is completing work at a pace that is faster than originally planned

For those interested in extending out the EVM concept to forecasting performance metrics into the future, there are a couple of methods for accomplishing that task. Caution should be used, however, when using simple formulas to predict future estimates as they contain an inherent assumption that conditions that currently exist within the project will continue to exist for the duration of the project, which may or may not be true. With that caveat extended, the following represent the simple formulas to calculate forecast-based scenarios: (note that data-based examples reference the sample data values in Figure 28:

A. Estimate At Completion (EAC) = $AC + \frac{(BAC - EV)}{CPI}$

   a. Sample: EAC = $50 + \frac{(105 - 45)}{0.9}$ or 116.67 *Total Hours*

B. Estimate To Complete (ETC) = $EAC - AC$

a.   Sample: ETC = 116.67 − 50 or 66.67 Hours Remaining

Earned Value Analysis (with Tolerance Limiting)

An alternative method for charting earned value that has attracted recent attention in the visual project management community is a concept known as tolerance limiting.   This tool is traditionally used in quality control circles to represent the limitation of values between which measurements must lie if an item is to be considered "acceptable."

Tolerance limiting itself is derived from other quality control tools used frequently in Six Sigma methodology including variance tracking and control limits. In the measurement of any process, there is an expected value, or mean, in which the process is assumed to operate. Control limits are placed at pre-determined intervals on both sides of the mean. In Six Sigma, these intervals are based on the standard deviations of the mean. These limits are then used to detect events in a process that may indicate that the process is not in control and, therefore, not operating predictably.

Figure 29 - Sample Control Chart

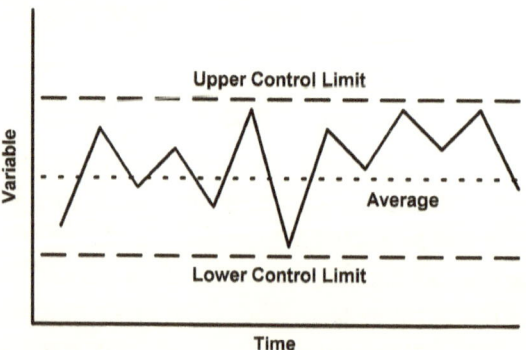

As steps in the process are completed, they are logged as an event. A variance signal is defined as any single event outside of the control limits, also known as a variance from the specified mean. A process is also considered out of control if there are seven consecutive points, still inside the control limits, but on one single side of the mean.

While the level of statistical rigor associated with quality control methodologies is not necessary for application in project management, this background in process control and tolerance limiting is important to understand when extending this concept to earned value analysis charting. Figure 30, shown below, depicts an earned value chart that includes upper and lower tolerance limits.

Figure 30 - Sample Earned Value Chart with Tolerance Limits

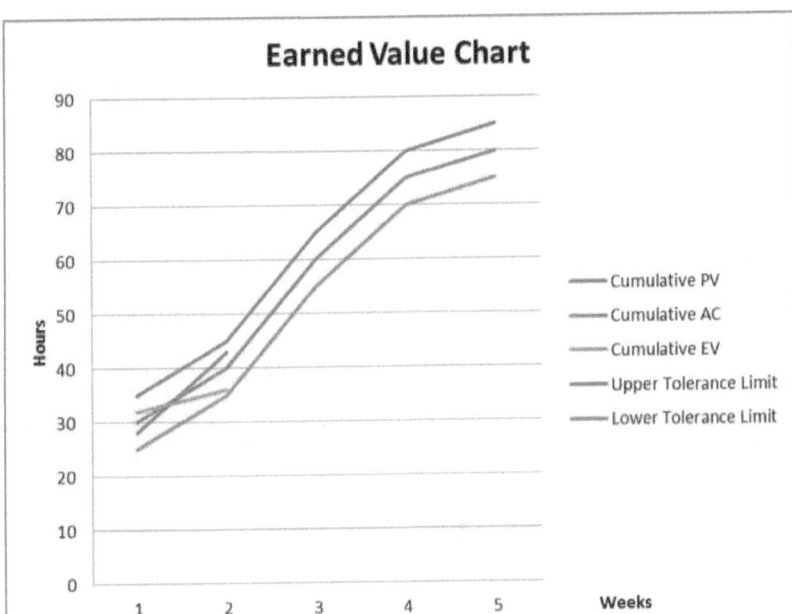

The three lines that parallel each other represent the cumulative planned value (middle line) and the corresponding upper and lower tolerance limits. Unlike usage of this concept in quality control circles, the limits are not based on statistically-driven guidelines such as standard deviations. Rather, the upper and lower limits are manually established by the project management office (PMO), project leadership team or key stakeholders based on risk tolerance, acceptance of minimal variation expected in project execution and other factors as determined by the appropriate governance body.

Think of tolerance limits as guardrails within which the project is expected to perform. If either the actual cost or earned value eclipse these tolerance limits, it serves as a trigger point to alert project management leadership that the project has deviated from the plan to an extent that certain action(s) must be taken. Sometimes that action is nothing more than to raise awareness, while in other circumstances, it requires additional analysis and/or mandatory meetings to review and discuss options for getting the project back on track.

As shown in Figure 30, the earned value is very nearly triggering the lower tolerance limit. This indicates that the project has fallen behind schedule to a point that has been previously determined as requiring additional attention. Compounding the issue on this particular example is the fact that the actual cost is also trending away from the planned value, showing an over budget condition, and something indicative of a project that may be out of control.

The key advantages of placing tolerance limits around earned value-based project performance indicators are two-fold. First, and similar to standard earned value charting, it provides an easy to understand visual representation of project performance rather than trying to make sense of numbers and formulas. Secondly, it provides a mechanism to pause project execution in the event that the actual performance exceeds pre-determined action thresholds. This provides the project leadership team with the opportunity to take corrective action before the issue gets further out of hand.

Using Earned Value in Project Management Practice:

1. Project Cost Performance
2. Project Schedule Performance
3. Project Status Reporting
4. Project Monitoring and Control

For additional information regarding Earned Value concepts[ix]:

General Information & Resources
Earned Value (Wikipedia):   en.wikipedia.org/wiki/Earned_value_management
Project Management Institute: www.pmi.org
US DoD EVM Division: www.acq.osd.mil/evm
Humpreys & Associates: www.humpreys-assoc.com/evms

Books
   Humphreys, Gary, *Project Management Using Earned Value.*
Humphreys and Associates, 2001, ISBN 978-0-970-86140-0
   Project Management Institute, *Practice Standard for Earned Value Management*, Project Management Institute, 2005, ISBN 978-1-930-69942-5
   Defense Contract Management Agency, "*Earned Value Implementation Guide,* DAU, 2006, ISBN 978-1-468-17828-9
   Fleming, Quentin, *Earned Value Project Management, Fourth Edition,* Project Management Institute, 2010, ISBN 978-1-935-58908-2

Popular Software Tools
Microsoft Excel® & Project®   office.microsoft.com
Deltek®   www.deltek.com/products/ppm/
Primavera®   www.oracle.com/applications/primavera
EcoSys™   www.ecosys.net

[ix] See Legal Disclaimer (pg. iv)

<u>Notes</u>

Dashboards

A dashboard is a collection of performance data, represented in graphical format, to provide an "at-a-glance," real-time snapshot of the health of a project, process or work unit. Dashboards are typically designed as a display of multiple data points such as text boxes, charts and other pictographic information, presented on a single page or electronic portal. They depict current status and historical trending of individual key performance indicators, along with other pertinent material that is used to support informed decision making.

Dashboards are referred to as such because they are modeled after automobile dashboards that contain gauges providing real-time information and feedback. Just as the displays on an automobile dashboard summarize the performance of hundreds of individual components and interconnections under the hood, business dashboards do the same for the dozens of individual business processes and performance metrics in the back offices of many organizations.

The first use of dashboards appear within the public utility and space industries in the 1950s and were designed to provide instant "go/no go" decision making regarding the state of technical components. Dashboards, in the management information system sense, came into being in the 1970s as a delivery mechanism for a much larger organizational decision-making movement known as Decision Support Systems (DSS). Essentially, the original business dashboards were developed to provide a "single source of truth" representation of all the disparate data sources being captured for Executive Information Systems.

Most dashboards employ in their design a graphical device known as a "Stop Light" to communicate status and health at a glance. Green indicates all is well and proceeding as planned, yellow is used to trigger additional attention, indicate negative trending or solicit an action step, while red indicates the item being measured is in trouble, has stopped and/or requires immediate attention. Typically, these color-based states have pre-determined variance thresholds that indicate when a key performance metric moves through the color scheme.

Dashboards also commonly leverage some frequently used pictographs including bars, sliders, pie charts, dials, traffic lights, gauges, timelines, etc.

Figure 31 - Common Dashboard Pictographs

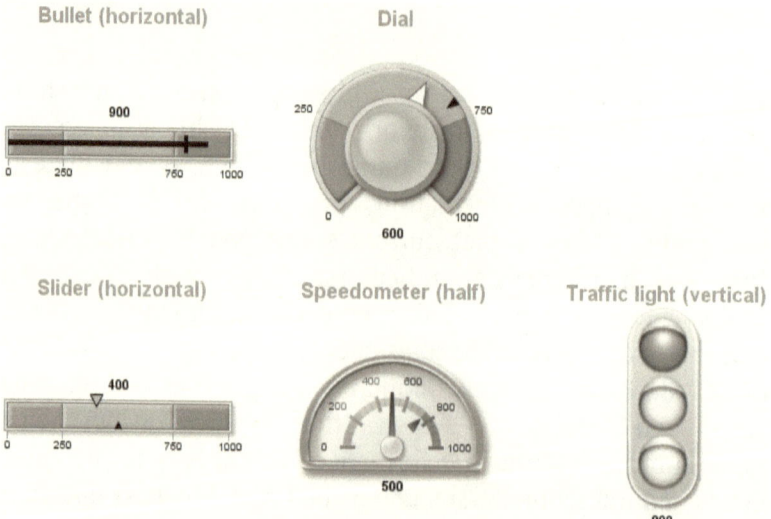

Foundationally and structurally, dashboard displays are made up of two essential components:

1. The Data Source: A database or source of key performance indicator data.
   a. Depending on the size and maturity of the organization, the data source can range from a simple spreadsheet grid, all the way up to purpose-built KPI management software suites which dynamically pull data from the organization's data warehouse.

2. The Data Display: A graphical method for displaying a particular data set.
   a. Most dashboards leverage charting software or functionality within a software program (eg. Microsoft Excel®)
   b. The data is displayed based on graphic type, max/min values, color coding, data positioning and data source

There are a number of important guidelines to keep in mind when designing and building a dashboard:

1. Design the dashboard for the intended audience
   a. Solicit the specific information and/or data points that are important to key stakeholders, leaders and other consumers of the dashboard and ask them what data helps them make decisions
   b. Come to consensus on the KPIs, data sources and display types across all stakeholders where possible
2. Keep the dashboard clutter-free
   a. Make the dashboard professional, visually attractive and easy to digest for quick understanding of status or performance
   b. Resist the temptation to add anything more than is needed just because the data exists
3. Decide on the logistics of the dashboard
   a. Consistent layout and format
      i. Design parameters:
         1. Scope: Broad vs. Specific
         2. Focus: Strategic vs. Operational
         3. Timeline: Historical vs. Real-Time
         4. Detail: Summary or Drill-Down
      ii. Each release of the dashboard should have the same presentation layout...only the data should change
   b. When is the dashboard released and reviewed?
      i. Is the dashboard:
         1. Published in a common location
         2. Distributed electronically

3. Distributed as part of a meeting or review session
4. Available online
   ii. What is the release schedule?
  c. How often is the data is refreshed?
     i. Does the dashboard need to reflect real-time status or is it a reflection of the data in the last week, month, quarter, etc.?

Dashboards provide a number of key benefits in presenting vital information in a quick, easily digestible format, including:

- Simplification of complex performance measurement formulas and statistically-driven data sources
- Ability to quickly identify outliers and correct negative trends
- Ability to see correlations and trending in data
- Alignment of strategy and goals to quantitative performance measurements
- Single-source data collection and reporting to avoid "dirty," duplicate or out of sequence data
- Time savings on report generation activities

The use of dashboards in project management practice is a natural fit. Sharing vital project performance metrics in a concise and consistent manner is a key communication responsibility of all project managers. While not appropriate for all project reporting needs, a dashboard is ideal for communicating at a higher, summary level.

Quite frankly, the easiest way to learn about dashboards, and the different options available in representing data visually, is to simply study various examples. The reader is strongly encouraged to take advantage of the myriad of examples published online for review and further study. To provide some reference to the topic, the next six pages include a sampling of project management-related dashboards.

Figure 32 - Sample Status Report Dashboard

WEEKLY PROJECT STATUS REPORT DASHBOARD

				Go-Live Date	02-12-14	Period End	11-20-13
Project	Project X	Phase:	Planning	Schedule(R)	Scope(G)	Budget(R)	Issues(Y)
Sponsor		Business Lead	IT Lead		PM Lead		

Sponsor Action Requested

Sponsor Awareness

△ Decisions Needed

△ △ FYI

Accomplishments Last Period

Goals Next Period

△ Item 1 △ △ Goal 1

△ Item 2 △ △ Goal 2

△ Item 3 △ △ Goal 3

Key Milestones (Next Six Weeks)

	Baseline Finish	Planned Finish
Milestone 1	10/05/13	11/06/13(R)
Milestone 2	10/18/13	11/25/13(R)
Milestone 3	11/25/13	12/08/13(Y)
Milestone 4	11/15/13	11/15/13(G)
Milestone 5	11/25/13	11/20/13(G)

Top 5 Issues

	Priority	Target Date	Assigned To
#1 Issue	High	11/15/13	
#2 Issue	Medium	12/15/13	
#3 Issue	Low	12/07/13	
#4 Issue	Low	02/04/14	
#5 Issue	Low	01/18/14	

Budget (From Business Case)	Actual (OpEx + CapEx)	Remaining Spend (Budget - Actual)	Spend-to-Date % (Budget / Actual)	Forecast (Estimate At Complete)	Variance (Forecast - Budget)	Variance % (Forecast / Budget)
$0	$0	$0	0%	$0	$0	0%

Figure 33 - Sample Project Approval Dashboard

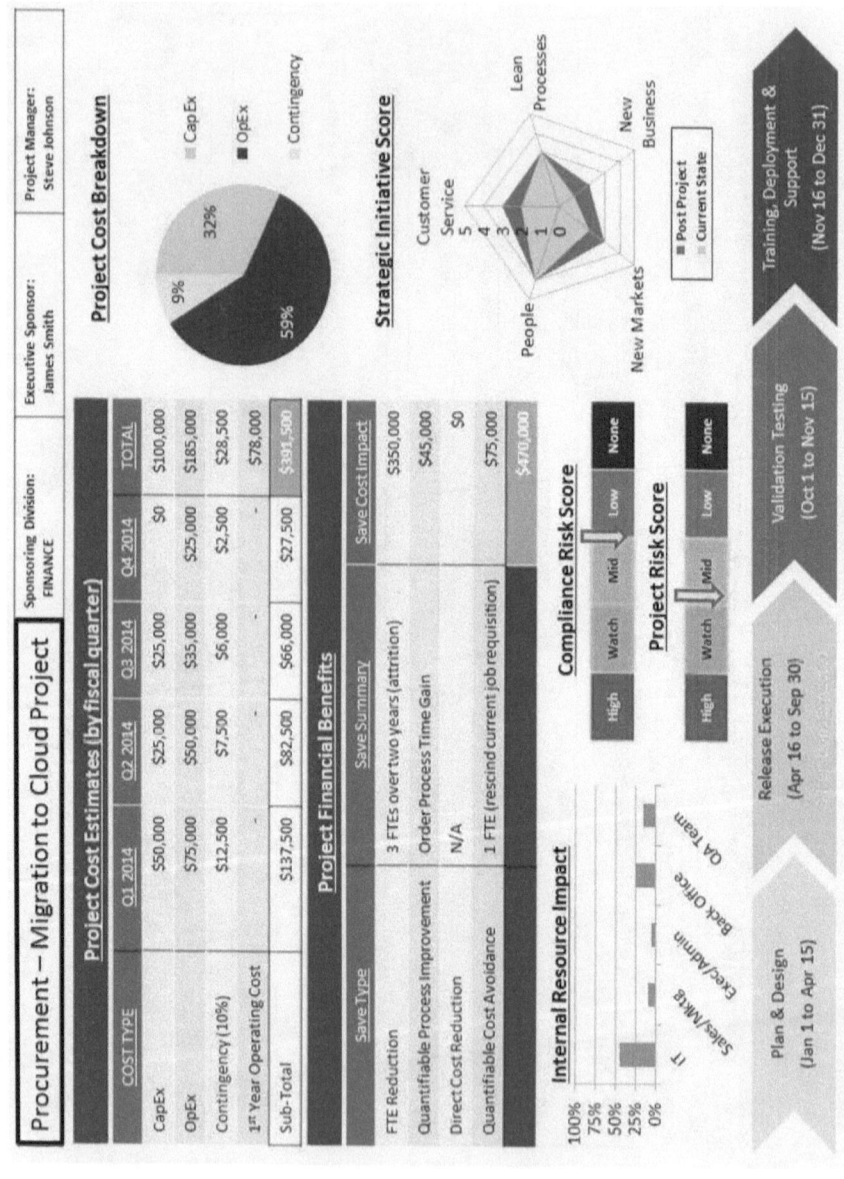

Figure 34 – Sample Program Level Dashboard

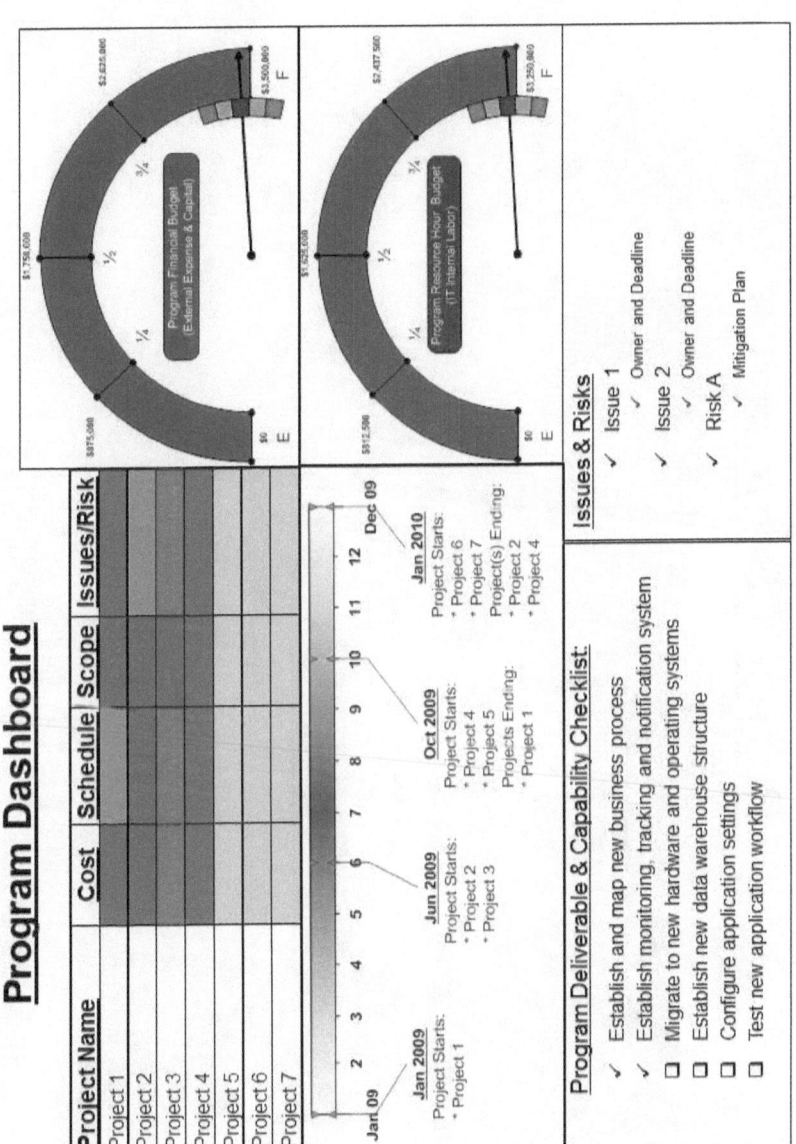

Figure 35 – Sample Project Scorecard Dashboard

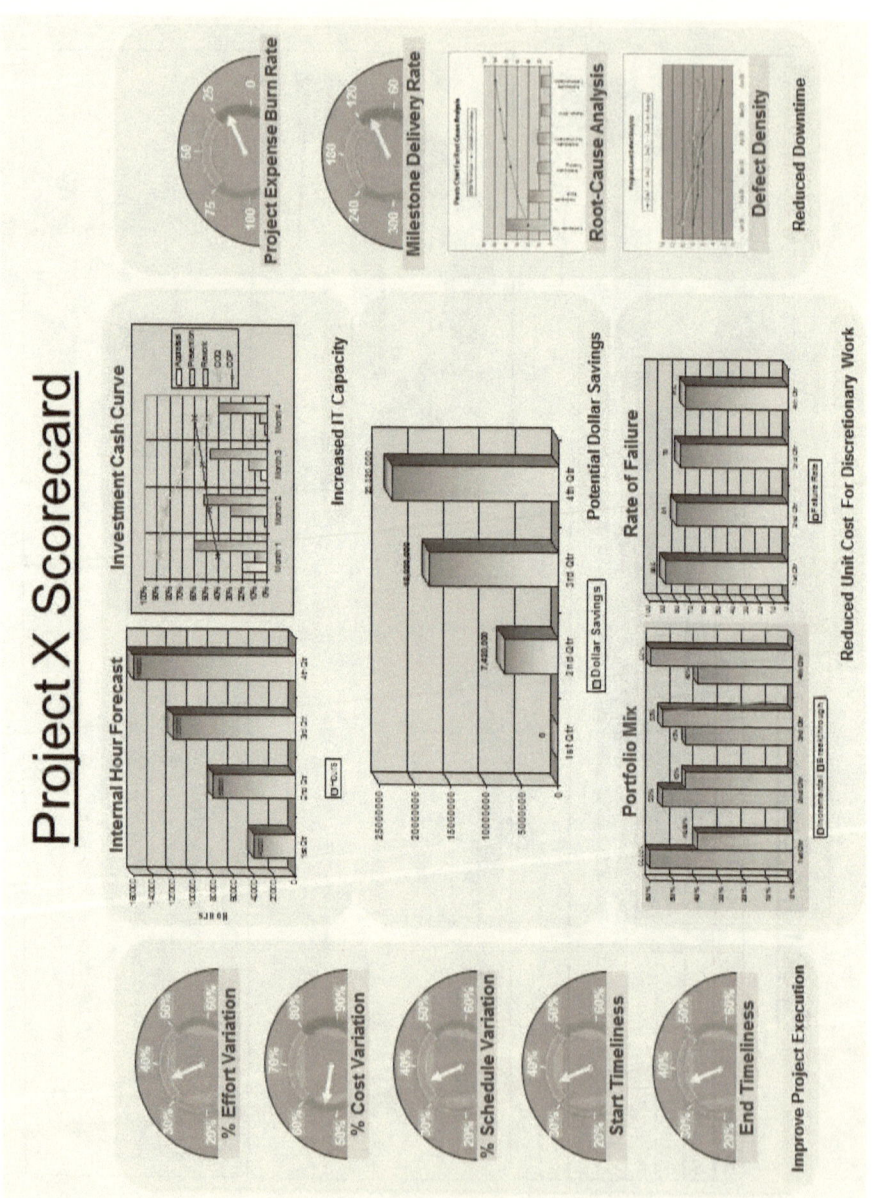

Figure 36 - Sample Project Health Check Dashboard

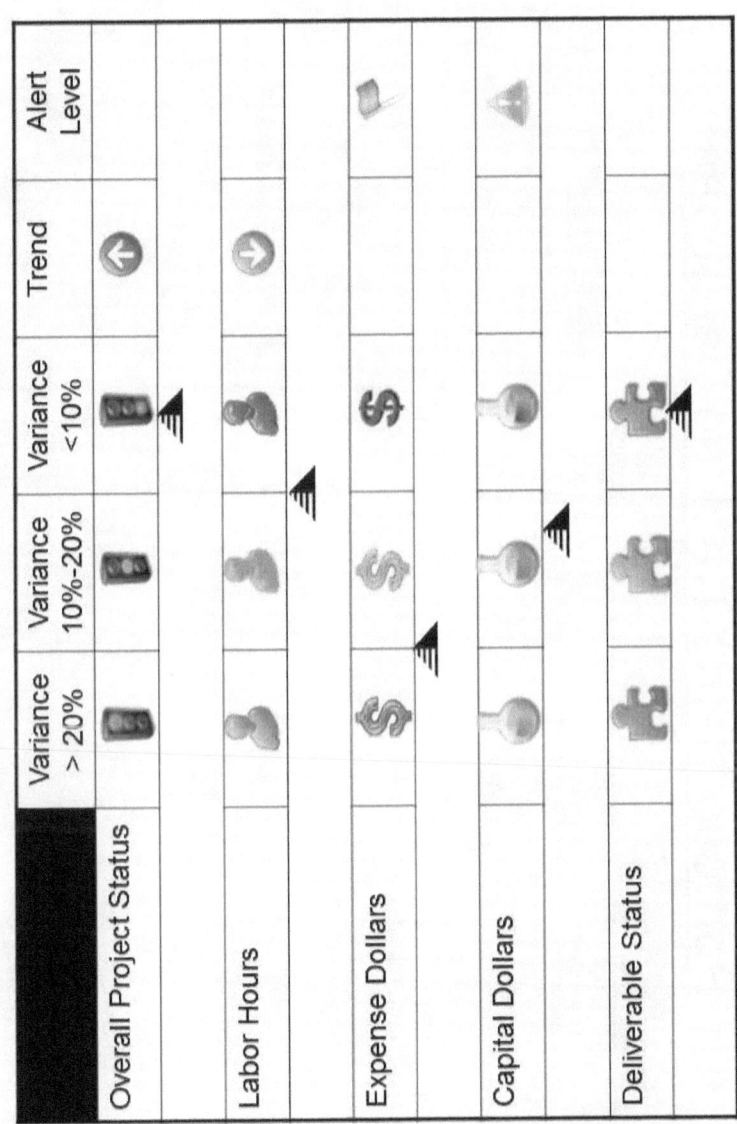

Figure 37 - Sample Portfolio Metric Tracking Dashboard

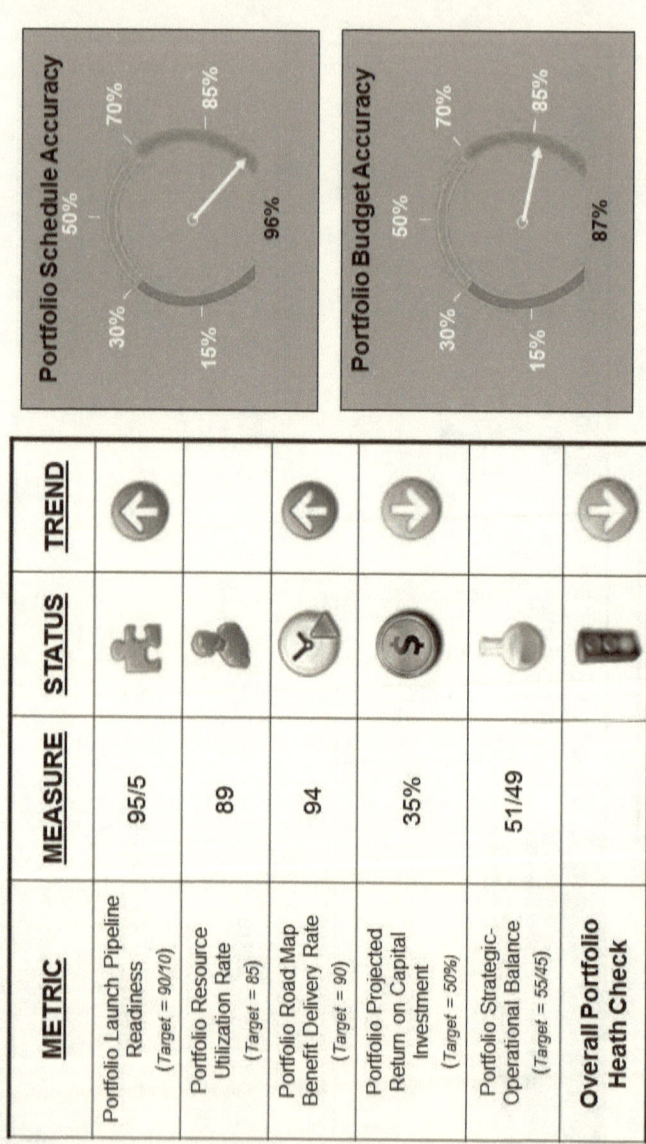

Portfolio Metric Tracking Dashboard

METRIC	MEASURE	STATUS	TREND
Portfolio Launch Pipeline Readiness (Target = 90/10)	95/5		
Portfolio Resource Utilization Rate (Target = 85)	89		
Portfolio Road Map Benefit Delivery Rate (Target = 90)	94		
Portfolio Projected Return on Capital Investment (Target = 50%)	35%		
Portfolio Strategic-Operational Balance (Target = 55/45)	51/49		
Overall Portfolio Heath Check			

Portfolio Schedule Accuracy
50%
70%
85%
30%
15%
96%

Portfolio Budget Accuracy
50%
70%
85%
30%
15%
87%

Using Dashboards in Project Management Practice:

1. Project Status Reporting
2. Project Monitoring and Control
3. Project Communications
4. Stakeholder Decision Making

For additional information regarding Dashboarding concepts[x]:

General Information & Resources
Google Image Search for Project Dashboard Examples: images.google.com
Dimensional Insight Dashboard Design 101:   www.dimins.com
One-Page Project Manager (Resources):   www.oppmi.com

Books
      Eckerson, Wayne, *Performance Dashboards: Measuring, Monitoring and Managing Your Business*, Wiley, 2010, ISBN 978-0-470-58983-0
      Few, Stephen, *Information Dashboard Design: The Effective Visual Communication of Data*, O'Reilly Media, 2006, ISBN 978-0-596-10016-2
      Kerzner, Harold, *Project Management Metrics, KPIs and Dashboards: A Guide to Measuring and Monitoring Project Performance*, Wiley, 2013 ISBN 978-1118-52466-4
      Campbell, Clark and Campbell, Mick, *The New One-Page Project Manager: Communicate and Manage Any Project with A Single Sheet of Paper*, Wiley, 2012, ISBN 978-1-118-37837-3

Popular Software Tools
Klipfolio™   www.klipfolio.com
iDashboards™   www.idashboards.com
Domo Business Dashboards™   www.domo.com
ConceptDraw®   www.conceptdraw.com

---

[x] See Legal Disclaimer (pg. iv)

<u>Notes</u>

Road Maps

The exercise of "road mapping" is the development of a timeline-based plan that aligns strategic goals, across many time horizons, with specific action plans, projects and/or technologies that will deliver upon the defined goals. As a graphical representation of the framework for the delivery of multiple interdependent platforms such as technology, product development, marketing, sales, etc., the road map serves as a guidepost to ensure that the entire organization remains aligned, over time, to both the larger, over-arching strategic goals and the smaller (relatively), tactical completion of the individual road map components.

Pioneered by Motorola in the 1970s, road maps were developed to encourage strategic alignment, dialogue and product planning across all functions within the organization, most notably work that had traditionally been independently planned and managed by the separate business units. Road mapping brings together functional experts from each business process and, using a set of graphical tools and templates, visualize and develop strategies, goals, interactions and deliverables for the road map.

Road mapping exercises, and the physical creation of the road map artifacts themselves, are distinctly different from developing project plans. In project plan development, emphasis is placed on executing a definable, singular piece of work. The focus of project-based planning is primarily on task sequence and execution, resource planning and utilization, along with cost, schedule and scope-based constraints. Road maps, on the other hand, essentially reverse this focus by asking individual business units to think about, and convey, how their goals, plans and actions fit within the context of the entire organization's goals and objectives. In this sense, road mapping and road maps help to link actions with strategic alignment and direction.

The concepts and approach behind building a good road map are flexible enough to be customized across a number of different business unit uses:

- Strategy Development
- Product Development
- Technology Planning
- New Business Development
- Services & Capabilities Planning
- Process Planning
- Integration Planning

In order to develop a road map, the team must first break down higher-order systems into subsystems and then ultimately into individual components. It is at this component level that the road map is generated so that individual components can be interchanged, re-sequenced or added/removed as the right balance is sought for the overall road map. Conducting these alternative scenario exercises allow for additional analysis regarding the potential impact that each alternative, or combination of alternatives, will have on the overall timing and/or effect of achieving the organization's strategic goals and objectives.

This decomposition of higher-order systems into sub-components is very similar to the project management activity of generating a work breakdown structure. In the case of the road map, however, the itemization of components is not centered on the work needed to produce the deliverable, but rather across business, product or technological lines. The visual nature of the road map clearly delineates when contributing components must be ready to support future events or coalesce in a specific order over time to meet the overall strategic goals at the end of the proposed timeline. (see Figure 38)

Figure 38 - Example Strategic Road Map

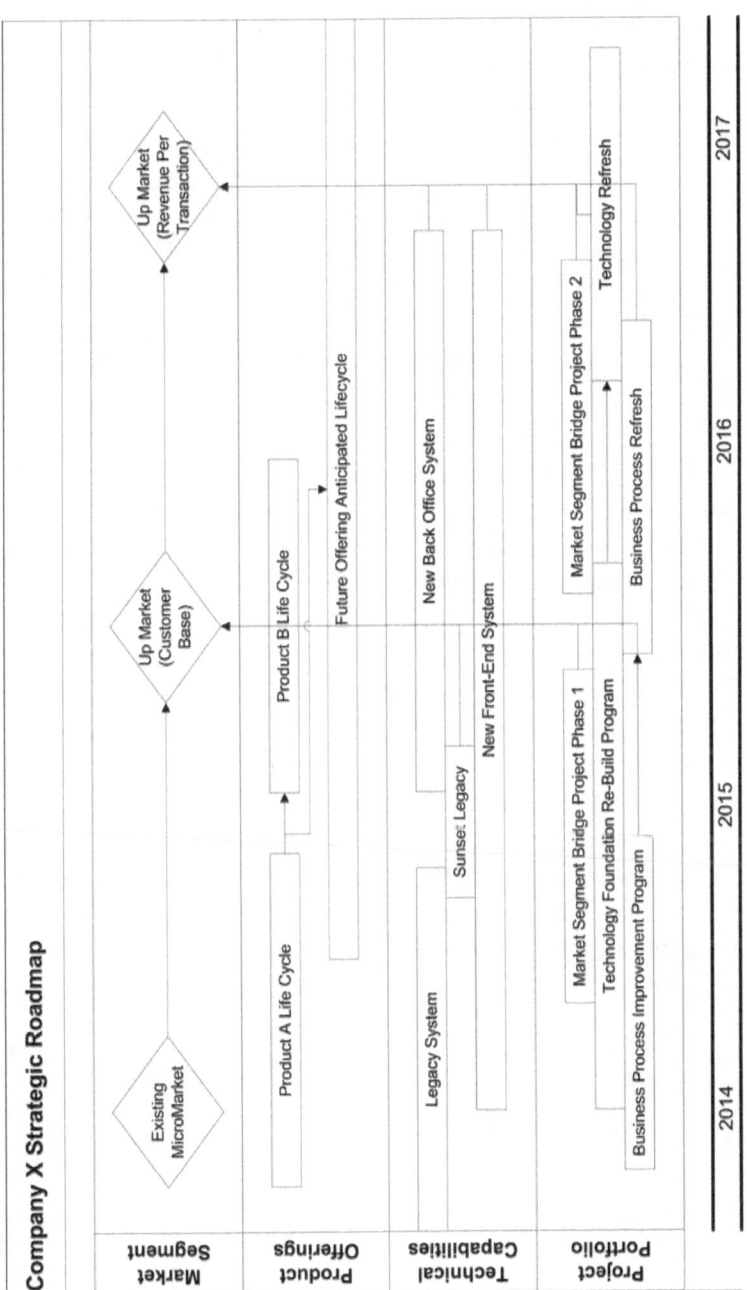

Road mapping workshops, and the road map documents they produce, have four main objectives:

1. Reach agreement on goals and objectives (current and future) of the organization
2. Break down the processes, technologies and other resources needed to achieve the goals and objectives identified
3. Seek to predict future developments and environmental changes that may affect the existing set of processes, technologies and resources
4. Build a tactical plan to integrate existing approaches with likely future scenarios, including strategic visions for process, technology and other resources

While the usage of road maps and road mapping techniques for the management of individual projects is not particularly common, they are occasionally used to show milestones or key deliverables, along with organizational resource dependencies, over time. Where road maps are quite useful in project management practice, however, is at the portfolio and/or program management tier.

Because project portfolios and programs need to take into account additional complexities such as market forces, technology stacks, business/manufacturing processes or product life cycles in order to make key prioritization and funding decisions, the usage of road maps help to bring order to the multiple pieces that make up the overall organizational strategic and execution puzzle. When done correctly, road maps are uniquely powerful, visual-based collaboration and decision support tools that align technology choices to business objectives, govern project selection, and guide project portfolio prioritization discussions.

Figure 39 - Sample Project Portfolio Road Map

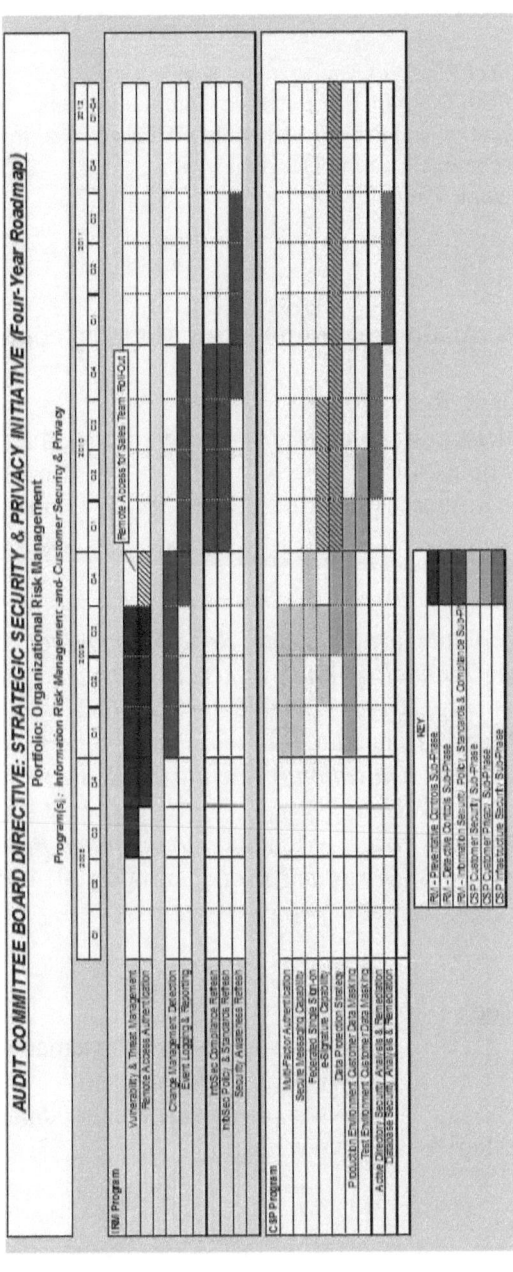

Using Road Maps in Project Management Practice:

1. Project Portfolio Management & Planning
2. Project, Program and Portfolio Communications
3. Executive and Project Stakeholder Decision Making
4. Resource Allocation Decision Making
5. Strategic Planning

For additional information regarding Road Mapping concepts[xi]:

General Information & Resources
Developing & Implementing Road Maps – A Reference Guide by Irene Petrick (via Penn State & Sopheon)[33]
Road Mapping 101 Resource (including references) by Global NP Solutions[34]

Books
        Phaal, Robert and Farrukh, Clare, *Road Mapping for Strategy and Innovation: Aligning Technology and Markets in a Dynamic World*, Univ. of Cambridge Inst. For Mfg, 2010, ISBN 978-1-902-54682-7
        Moehrle, Martin, Isenmann, Ralf and Phaal, Robert, *Technology Road Mapping for Strategy and Innovation: Charting the Route to Success*, Springer, 2013, ISBN 978-3-642-33922-6
        Daim, Tugrul and Pizarro, Melinda, *Planning and Road Mapping Technological Innovations: Cases and Tools*, Springer, 2014. ISBN 978-3-319-02972-6

Popular Software Tools
Sopheon®   www.sopheon.com/roadmapping-software/
ProductPlan™   www.productplan.com
Planisware™   www.planisware.com/roadmapping
Aha! Visual Road Map™   www.aha.io

[xi] See Legal Disclaimer (pg. iv)

Lean Concepts - Kanban

Because a great deal of academic study and superb business writing regarding the subject of leveraging lean manufacturing concepts, including Kanban, for business operations, process improvement and project management already exists, this chapter will focus primarily on the visual tools used within Kanban systems. More specifically, this chapter will explore how Kanban-based tools can be leveraged in project management discipline, especially for the visual management of task execution and resource capacity.

As background for readers who may not be familiar with the history of lean manufacturing concepts, the origin of Kanban takes its roots back to the early 1940s and Sakichi Toyoda. While researching methods to make his Toyota Industries manufacturing operations more efficient, Toyoda started studying shelf-stocking techniques used by local grocery stores as a possible solution to inventory control and timely part stocking on his factory floor. In his analysis Toyoda learned that grocery stores stock only what they expect to sell within a given time frame, while customers take only what they need for a given time, since there is no need to stockpile goods as future supply is assured. This observation led Toyoda to view this interchange as a process where the "customer" (line worker) goes to the store to obtain required components, which in turn causes the "store" (parts supply area) to restock. This process came to be known as "Just-in-Time" (JIT) inventory control.

The name 'Kanban' originates from Japanese, and translates roughly to "signboard" or "billboard". Kanban was developed by a Toyota Industries employee, Taiichi Ohno, as a system to improve and maintain a high level of production.[35]   A Kanban system maintains inventory levels by monitoring, in real-time, available inventory on the factory floor. As the inventory is reduced, a pre-determined threshold is eclipsed which triggers a signal back to the procurement process or system to produce and/or deliver a new shipment of inventory. Ideally, the new inventory arrives "just-in-time," or as the existing stock is exhausted. In essence, Kanban uses the rate of demand or consumption to control the rate of production or delivery, better known in lean circles as "work-in-progress."

In knowledge-based work such as software development, Kanban is a method for controlling work-in-progress so as to avoid overloading development teams.   Additionally, the use of Kanban outside of the factory floor is much more visually-oriented. In fact, the entire work process, from creation of a task to its eventual delivery to the end-user, is displayed for stakeholders to view and for execution team members to pull work from a centralized queue. Kanban, in this sense, is essentially a visual process management system that tells people what to produce, when to produce it, and how much to produce, in order to control it through work management systems.

Modern usage of Kanban for knowledge work was developed by David J. Anderson[36] as an approach to incremental, evolutionary process and systems change for organizations. It uses a work-in-progress limited pull system as the core mechanism to expose system operation (or process) problems and stimulate collaboration to continuously improve the system.[37]

The use of visualization is critical in Kanban-based systems. Without knowing what the work looks like, how that work moves through the process, what actions are required or what dependencies exist, it becomes difficult to measure progress or improve performance of the process. As a key tool in another popular business management concept known as "visual control," information is communicated within the Kanban system through the use of visual signals instead of text or other written instructions. These visual techniques, such as sticky notes on a whiteboard that create a "picture" of the work or through the use of electronic Kanban boards, depict how the work flows within the process and facilitates communication of overall status. Additional details such as issues that are being worked by the team, work that has been completed or placed on hold, or identifying who is responsible for which tasks in the process are also made clear by viewing the Kanban board.

Before Kanban, this information was presented in static status reports or Gantt charts. After Kanban, the work becomes visual and available real-time.

Kanban systems have four main doctrines:

1. Visualize the Work Flow
   a. Create the visual model of the workflow and the tasks within that workflow
   b. Separate work across individual "states of work" columns (Not Started, In Progress, Complete, etc.)
   c. Use individual cards, sticky notes, etc. to indicate a particular task in the system
   d. Move the cards/notes across the board as work is pulled and completed
2. Limit Work-In-Progress (WIP)
   a. Set limits on how much unfinished work can exist in the process to control the flow of work
   b. Follows a concept known as "Little's Law"[38], which uses a queueing mathematical theory that identifies the ideal capacity any system can hold before bottlenecks, undesired queue levels or process blocks begin to form within the process
   c. Work that does become a bottleneck is also instantly visible which leads to better communication and action
3. Work is "Pull-Based"
   a. Assumes all tasks within system are equal and do not have dependencies on each other (unless noted)
   b. Allows for work to be pulled from the backlog in any order, which facilitates task switching as needed and reduces the need to constantly reprioritize items
4. Work Focus is on the Flow
   a. Work-in-progress limits should optimize flow
   b. Collect metrics to understand how to set WIP limits
   c. Experiment with queueing (upstream) limits to prevent WIP overflow

In Figure 40, a very simple Kanban board is displayed to help orient the reader to the general concept. In this simple, three-column example, individual tasks are listed from A through J. At the onset of the work effort, all of the tasks would have been listed under the 'Backlog/To-Do' category. To keep the example simple, assume that Task A was the first task "pulled" by a resource to start work on the project. That resource would have moved the card or sticky note to the 'In-Progress' category so that anyone viewing the board could see it had been started. When the work was completed, the Task A card was moved to the 'Done' column on the Kanban board. The remaining tasks on the board will move through the system in a similar fashion.

In more sophisticated Kanban systems, the cards or sticky notes will likely have additional information listed on them that may include who is working on the task, an estimate of the work effort or duration, priority (sometimes signified by color-coding) and/or start date.

Figure 40 - Simple Kanban Board

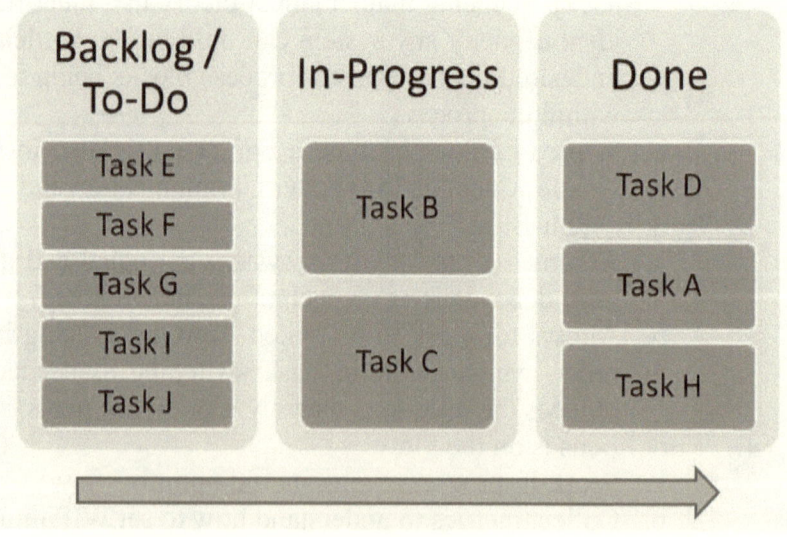

On even more advanced Kanban boards, additional features and functionality are added to include WIP limits, tasks that are blocked, tasks that need attention, additional staging "states" like 'Ready' or 'Next' to better manage waiting queues. (see Figure 41)

Figure 41 - Advanced Kanban Board (*made using LeanKit[39])

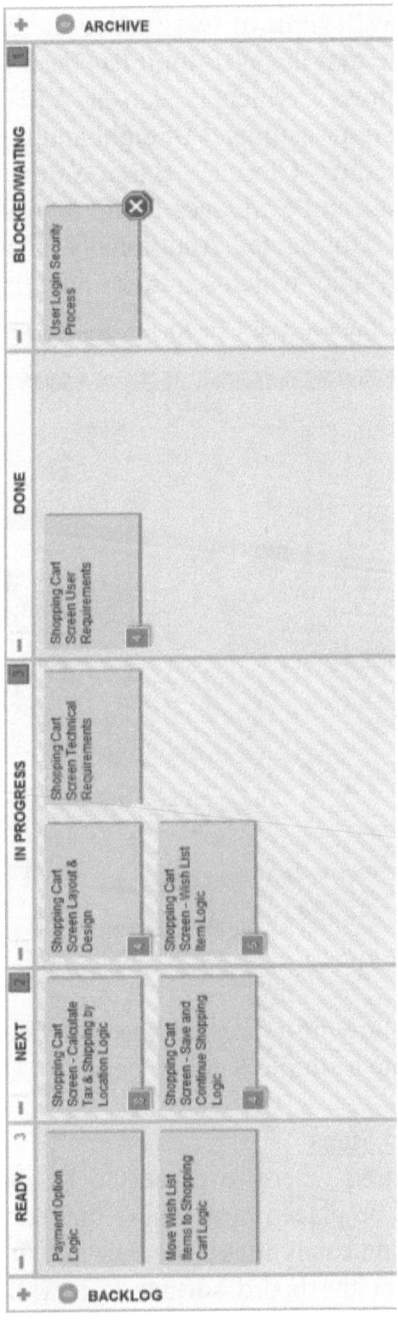

Using Figure 41 as reference, all tasks have been moved out of the 'Backlog.' Two tasks are waiting in the 'Ready' state, and the 'Next' state has reached its WIP limit of two (notice the hashing in the column background to indicate that the WIP limit has been reached). Three tasks are currently 'In-Progress,' which is also at WIP limit and two of the tasks have been given hour estimates of eight and four respectively. Only one task has been listed as 'Closed.' Based on the current status of this sample board, no tasks can be advanced until at least one task that is 'In-Progress' is moved to 'Complete.' Additionally, a task has been placed in the 'Blocked/Waiting' state, which requires immediate attention.

Figure 42 - Photo of Actual Kanban Board for Knowledge Work[40]

Finally, the following represent best-practice instructions and tips regarding how to create a simple Kanban board.

Recommended Steps:
1. Determine where to place the Kanban board. Ideally, it should be placed near where the team doing the work can see it and easily make changes and updates.
2. Whether the board surface is a wall, a whiteboard or an easel pad, mark out the columns that represent the "states"

that the tasks will move through. At the most basic level, these would minimally be: Backlog, In-Progress and Done. Add columns that are appropriate for organizing work that may have unique category states.

3. Using index cards or sticky notes, create a card for each task in the process. Using a black permanent marker is recommended to make the task easily readable when placed on the board. Include any additional information on the card that is useful for the team, such as: person responsible, date started, expected finish date, effort estimate, etc.

4. Place the task cards in the appropriate column.

5. Arrange the task cards using some kind of prioritization system (if necessary).

Helpful Tips:

1. The same Kanban board can be used for multiple processes or projects by using different colored cards/sticky notes or different colored writing on the cards

2. Use team member photos to easily demonstrate who is working on what tasks

3. Consider adding an "expedited" lane that allows for emergency work to travel across the Kanban board outside of normal WIP limitations

4. Use red or yellow or orange cards/sticky notes to depict tasks that are in-trouble, need attention or are high-priority

Using Kanban in Project Management Practice:

1. Visual Workflow Management
2. Resource Capacity/Management
3. Process Improvement Initiatives

For additional information regarding Kanban concepts[xii]:

General Information & Resources
David J. Anderson & Associates: www.djaa.com
Toyota Global – Just-in-Time & Kanban: bit.ly/XEjBZl (*case sensitive*)
Personal Kanban: www.personalkanban.com

Books
      Anderson, David J., *Kanban: Successful Evolutionary Change for Your Technology Business*, Blue Hole Press, 2010, ISBN 978-0-984-52140-1
      Kniberg, Henrik, *Lean from the Trenches: Managing Large-Scale Projects with Kanban*, Pragmatic Bookshelf, 2011, ISBN 978-1-934-35685-2
      DeMaria Barry, Tonianne and Benson, Jim, *Personal Kanban: Mapping Work | Navigating Life*, CreateSpace, 2011, ISBN 978-1-453-80226-7

Popular Software Tools
LeanKit®   www.leankit.com
Rally®   www.rallydev.com
Kanbanize™   www.kanbanize.com
Trello®   www.trello.com

[xii] See Legal Disclaimer (pg. iv)

Agile Concepts – Scrum Visuals

Scrum Overview

Similar to the previous chapter, a wealth of information is readily available in both print and electronic formats regarding the usage, benefits and potential drawbacks of leveraging agile development methodology as a practice for delivering project-based outcomes. As was the approach in discussing Kanban, this chapter will not focus on the "how-to" of agile and/or Scrum in particular. Rather, the focus will be on the use of visual tools within the Scrum methodology and how those tools may be of benefit in general project management practice. The following brief overview is offered, however, to provide a basic foundation of agile and Scrum concepts for better comprehension of the visual tools used within the methodology.

It is important to note that there is a fundamental difference between Kanban and Scrum. Kanban was made popular in the modern lean manufacturing movement of the 1970s and 1980s and has as its primary focus the visualization of workflow and limitation of work-in-progress to improve process and inventory efficiency. Scrum, on the other hand, is rooted in both product and software development backgrounds and places its emphasis on time-boxing smaller "chunks" of work among self-organizing development teams. The two terms are often erroneously used as synonyms. Much of the confusion appears to stem from the Scrum methodology's use of a task board, which is very similar in appearance to a Kanban board, but is used in a much different manner.

Scrum is an iterative, incremental agile software development framework that takes its lead from the foundational principles set forth in the Agile Manifesto[41] for managing product and software development projects. The Agile Manifesto, and its underlying set of principles, centers around the reality that business requirements and technical solutions evolve through iterative collaboration between self-organizing, cross-functional teams during the life cycle of the project effort. Rather than depending on securing all of the necessary information before moving to the next step in the process, also known as "waterfall," agile methodology instead *"promotes adaptive planning, evolutionary development, early delivery, continuous improvement and encourages rapid and flexible response to change."*[42]

Ken Schwaber and Jeff Sutherland, are both considered the "founding fathers" of what is known today as Scrum. Although they did not work for the same organization, they jointly developed a presentation for the 1995 Object-Oriented Programming, Systems, Languages & Applications (OOPSLA) Conference in Austin, Texas that introduced the Scrum concept. From this foundation, the methodology, tools and techniques used in this approach have been matured and championed by an organization known as the Scrum Alliance.

In short, Scrum describes a product development strategy that encourages teams to self-organize, including the recommendation to physically or electronically co-locate team members. Work is accomplished in "sprints," which are time-boxed periods of work effort that produce working code, or a product component, at the end of the sprint. Team members independently select tasks to work on and provide a continuous estimate of how much work remains until that task is completed. As a self-directed group, team members hold each other accountable via daily "stand-up" meetings among all team members and representative disciplines in the project effort, with each team member answering only three questions during the stand-up: What did you finish yesterday?; What are you working on today?; What is preventing you from completing any planned work?

Finally, work inside of the sprint is tracked using two visual management tools. First, individual tasks are represented on a Scrum Task Board, which is very similar in appearance to a Kanban board but with task states that align more appropriately to software development work. Second is the Sprint Burn-Down Chart, which visually depicts the remaining work in a plot chart format.

Scrum Task Board

A Scrum task board is a simple, visual reference of status for tasks that have been committed to as part of the current "sprint." Structured similar to a Kanban board (see page 92), it is a simple column-based, sectioned grid. On a typical Scrum board, the far left column is either titled, 'Backlog' or 'To-Do' and holds all of the task cards that have been created as part of the current sprint. The board is then bracketed by the column farthest to the right which is called, 'Done' and represents tasks that have been completed and/or released to production.

The number of columns between these two traditional Scrum board "states," and their titles, will vary widely based on organizational preferences for product and/or software development stages. Popular column states are listed here in work flow (left-to-right) order across the Scrum board:

- Backlog (defined above)
- Ready
  - Task has been defined and estimated
- Development In Progress
  - Represents tasks that are currently being worked or developed
- Development Complete
  - A queue area to indicate that the task is ready for system testing
- System Test
  - Tasks currently being system tested
- QA Validation/Code Review
  - Tasks currently undergoing a code review or other quality assurance validation
- Acceptance Testing In Progress
  - Tasks that are currently being acceptance tested (usually user acceptance or final acceptance testing)

- Acceptance Testing Complete
  - A queue area for tasks that can be scheduled as "ready" for promotion through the various technical environments
- Ready for Deployment/Stage
  - A queue area for tasks that are in the final pre-production environment and ready to be deployed
- Deployed/In Production/Done (defined above)

Figure 43 - Simple Scrum Task Board Example[43]

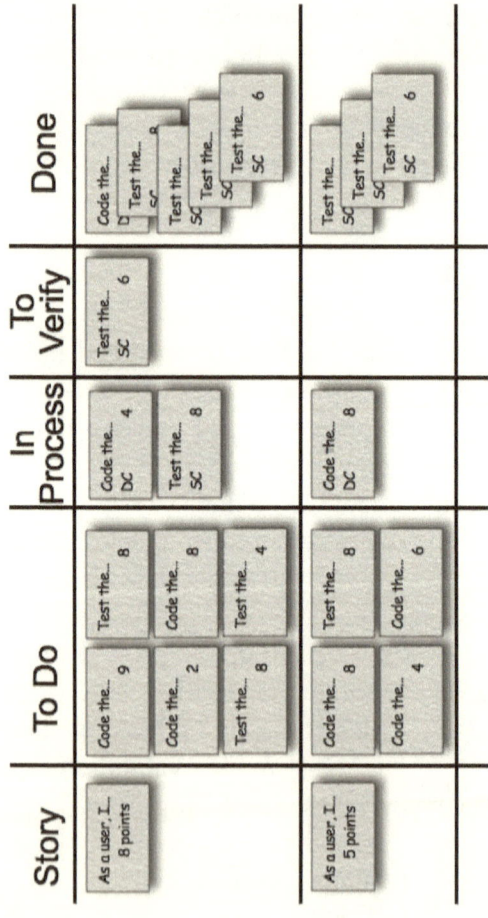

Figure 44 - Advanced Scrum Task Board Example

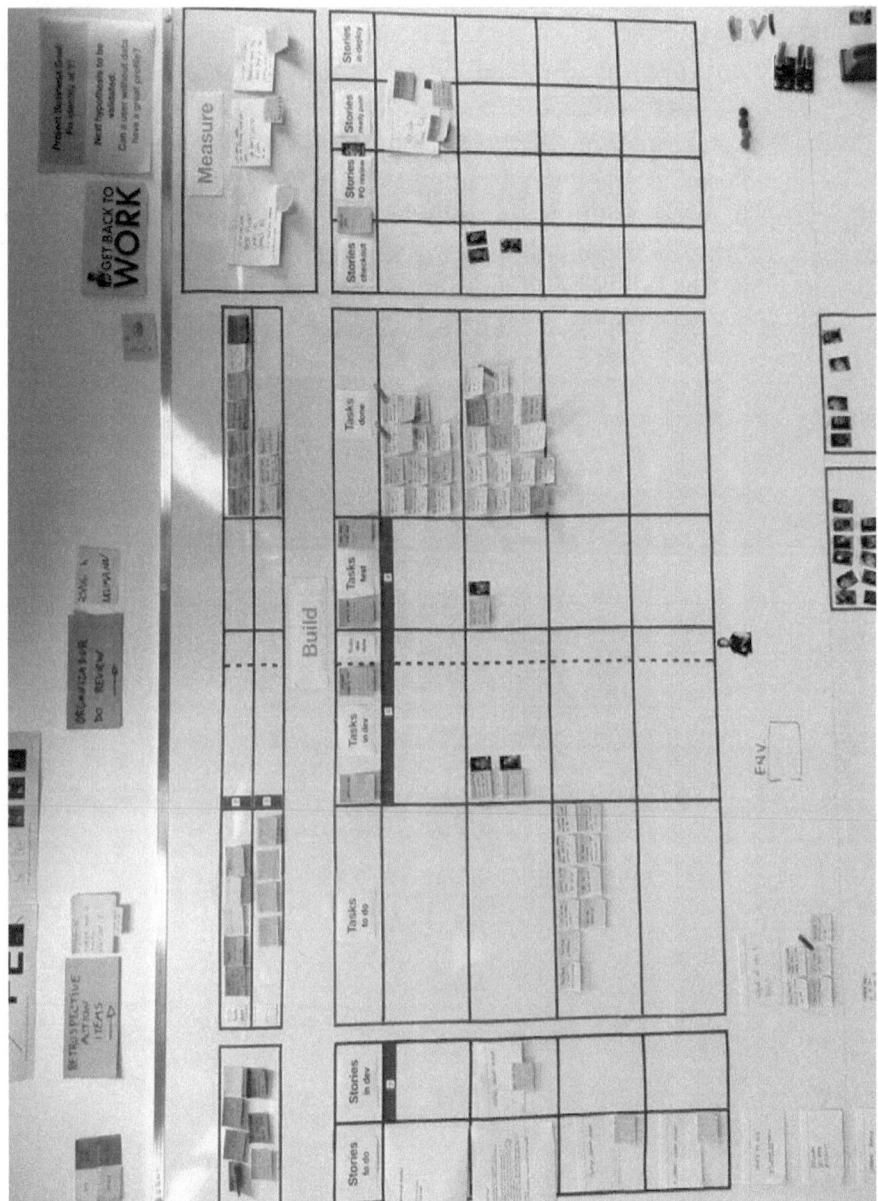

Scrum Sprint Burn-Down Chart

Shortly before each sprint begins, the team will analyze all of the product features (also referred to as User Stories) still available in the backlog and select the set of tasks that they will commit to completing during the coming sprint. After all of the tasks have been defined and the resource effort hours estimated, a sprint burn-down chart can be created to depict the total remaining effort until planned sprint closure.

The sprint burn-down chart is the visual representation of the comparison between the ideal burn-down path of remaining hours versus the actual burn-down path of remaining hours. This data is typically gathered in a chart that lists all tasks, the current status, owner of the task, date, beginning effort estimates and effort remaining. (see Figure 45)

Figure 45 - Sprint Burndown Chart Data Example

Task	Owner	Total Task Estimate	Days Remaining In Sprint										
			10	9	8	7	6	5	4	3	2	1	0
Task 1	PBarnett	16	16	14	10	8	6	4	0	0	0	0	0
Task 2	TKoenig	12	10	5	5	4	4	4	4	0	0	0	0
Task 3	CSmith	24	20	16	12	10	8	8	8	10	8	4	0
Task 4	JWilliams	8	8	4	4	0	0	0	0	0	0	0	0
Task 5	SHoltz	16	16	14	10	8	8	8	8	4	6	4	0
		76	70	53	41	30	26	24	20	14	14	8	0

Hours Remaining in Sprint

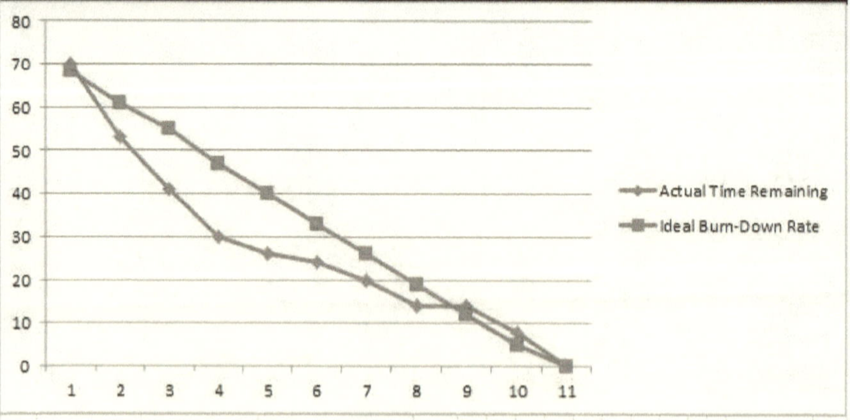

- Actual Time Remaining
- Ideal Burn-Down Rate

Figure 46 - Sprint Burndown Chart Example

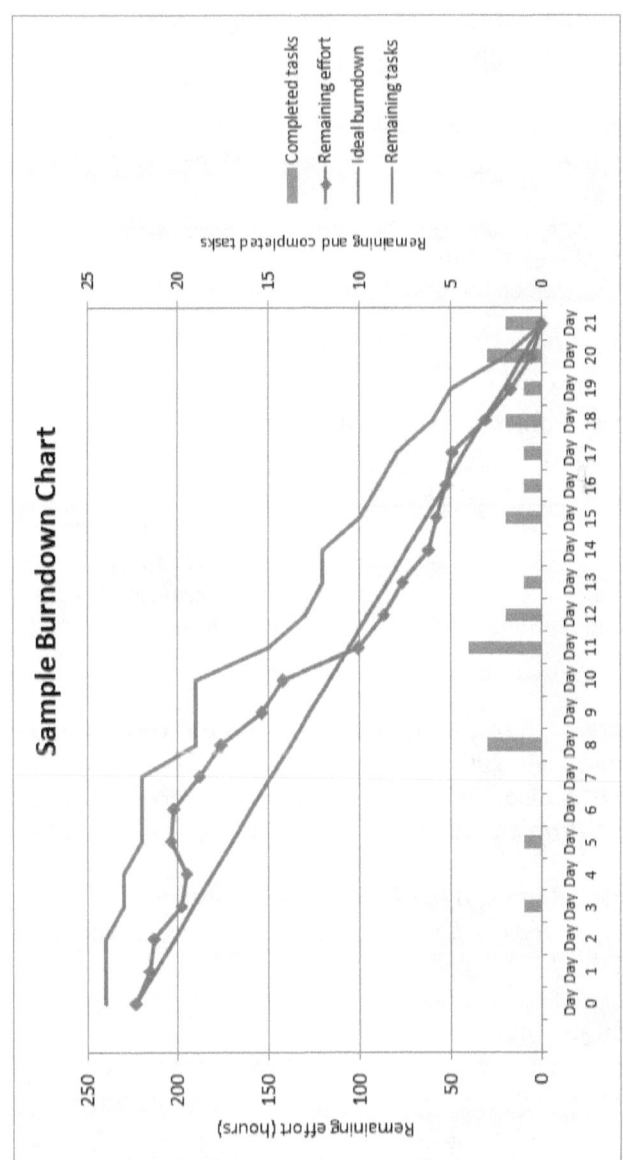

Burn-down charts are a very common companion next to any Scrum board so that, at a glance, it is easily discernable where tasks are in the process, how much work is left until completion and how that work is trending. Whether for use in a burn-down chart, or as a part of earned value calculations, tracking the estimated amount of work remaining is a valuable key metric and health indicator of project progress against plan.

Using Scrum Visual Tools in Project Management Practice:

1. Software/Product Development Project Management
2. Visual Workflow Management
3. Resource Capacity/Management

For additional information regarding Scrum Visual Tools[xiii]:

General Information & Resources
Scrum Alliance: www.scrumalliance.org
Scrum.org: www.scrum.org
Scrum Guides: www.scrumguides.com
Mountain Goat Software: www.mountaingoatsoftware.com

Books
        Schwaber, Ken and Beedle, Mike, *Agile Project Management with Scrum*, Prentice Hall, 2001, ISBN 978-0-130-67634-4
        Rubin, Kenneth, *Essential Scrum: A Practical Guide to the Most Popular Agile Process*, Addison-Wesley Professional, 2012, ISBN 978-0-137-04329-3
        Pichler, Roman, *Agile Product Management with Scrum: Creating Products that Customers Love*, Addison-Wesley Professional, 2010, ISBN 978-0-321-60578-8

Popular Software Tools
ScrumWise™   www.scrumwise.com
ScrumDesk™   www.scrumdesk.com
Axosoft®   www.axosoft.com
iScrumpad™   Apple® iOS App
AgileScrumPro ™   Apple® iOS App

[xiii] See Legal Disclaimer (pg. iv)

Infographics

Information graphics, more commonly referred to as 'infographics,' are graphical representations of data and information. They are created to communicate a concept or tell a story in an easy to comprehend and memorable visual format. Infographics represent the end product of the previously discussed larger field of study known as data visualization, which leverages the brain's natural ability to visually capture and neurally process images and patterns for better understanding of complex and/or disparate data sets.

Infographics have existed for hundreds of years in various forms or another. Early usage was typically limited to collections of statistical graphs and charts within publications such as an almanac, atlas or encyclopedic works. Infographics really caught on within the newspaper industry where they were (are) commonly used to show weather data, statistically-driven map displays known as cartograms, polling results, along with more traditional graphical representations of statistical data. A great example of newsprint usage of infographics is the daily 'Snapshot' that the USA Today™ uses to articulate current events or visually represent survey results.[44]

With the explosion of data sources available on the internet, inexpensive graphical design software, low cost (or even free) mobile apps and vast audiences available via social media, infographics have experienced a renaissance of late. What used to be the sole domain of graphical designers in news rooms or design shops has now been made available to the general public. These days, anyone can be an infographic designer.

The creation of effective infographics, however, requires a delicate balance between message delivery (presentation of the data) and message acceptance (the effectiveness of comprehension regarding the data).

Figure 47 - Infographic Design Balance

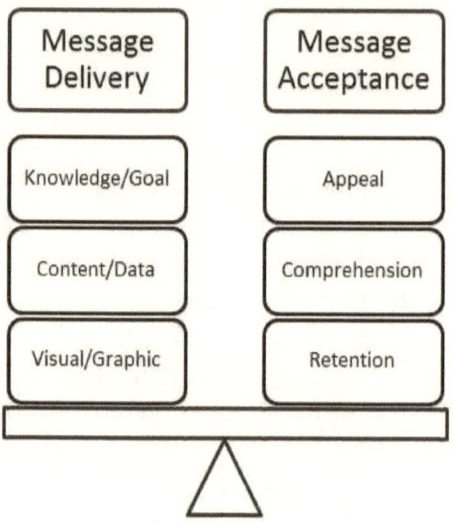

Focusing on the 'Message Delivery' side of the scale, represented in Figure 47, the visual aspect of infographic design consists of color and graphics choices. Typically, graphics are broken down into a couple of additional categories: theme-based graphics and reference-based graphics. Theme-based graphics represent the underlying visual representation of the data as a whole. Reference-based graphics, on the other hand, point only to certain data within the entire data set.

Content used in infographics come from statistics, facts and data points relevant to the topic being communicated. The information may come from private data sources such as project portfolio strategies, financial data or human resource databases. Information can also be obtained from a number of public sources, such as fact books, almanacs, census data, scientific studies or news outlets. Finally, the infographic must be created for a reason or purpose. What is the goal of sharing the data in this form? Proper infographic design must impart some knowledge with its intended audience.

On the 'Message Acceptance' side of the scale, the infographic must be designed to be appealing enough to capture the attention of the intended audience and engage them in the communication. Designing for comprehension validates that the viewer should be able to quickly and easily understand the information represented in the infographic. Lastly, the infographic needs to designed in such a way as to aid in memory recall and retention of the information being conveyed.

Generally speaking, there is no right or wrong way to balance delivery versus acceptance. In other words, some science is mixed in with the art. Some infographics used in textbooks or science journals focus more on comprehension and retention rather than visual appeal. Infographics developed for print and electronic news media are typically biased for appeal in order to capture attention, while infographics leveraged for business uses will combine appeal and comprehension to ensure the message is both heard and understood.

As for the actual creation of infographics, a myriad of tools ranging from simple drawings with pen and paper all the way to the other extreme of hiring an Infographic Design firm are readily available. With the recent surge in the popularity of infographics, a number of self-design tools have become available on the internet, via mobile apps and from downloadable software packages.

Additionally, while the structure and framing of the infographic itself may be facilitated by an end-to-end physical or electronic tool suite, the individual components that make up infographics, such as data sources, images, illustrations, label sets, vectors, icons and art stock, are also widely available in both free (for simple graphics) and royalty/per use fee-based (for professionally designed graphics) formats. More information regarding available infographic resources is listed at the end of this chapter and more broadly via internet search engines.

Please take special note that copyright laws exist world-wide and it is critical to consult these laws before using the work of another as part of any infographic. Additionally, take special care to properly follow accepted citation standards for any work used in an infographic that is not self-created. To help copyright owners manage their legal rights, a non-profit organization known as Creative Commons was founded to facilitate the legal sharing of creative works while allowing the creators to determine which rights they wish to reserve and which rights they may wish to waive. The Creative Commons group has also created a simple to use search engine to discover creative works that have been added to the public domain with the permission of the creator. In fact, some of the visualizations used in this work were discovered using the Creative Commons search page.

The use of infographics in project management practice is rapidly increasing as more and more project managers seek to communicate project status, performance metrics and complex information in a format that is quickly and easily digestible by their harried stakeholders, sponsors and oversight bodies. Some of the more traditional project management document artifacts that are being re-designed into infographic-form include:

- Project Status Reports
- Project Process Checklists
- Project Deliverable/Key Milestone Checklists
- Project Marketing Materials
- Project Stakeholder Briefings
- External Stakeholder/General Public Communications
- Project Risk Mitigation Plans
- Project Scope Definition Awareness

As the concept of visual thinking and the use of infographics continue to build momentum among the greater project management practitioner community, an increasing amount of traditional document artifacts and communication methodologies will take on a more infographic look and feel. The frenetic pace of business and the changing model of project oversight place increased demands on the project manager to communicate in a more concise and efficient manner, and infographics certainly appear to meet those criteria.

Figure 48 - Example Infographic[45]

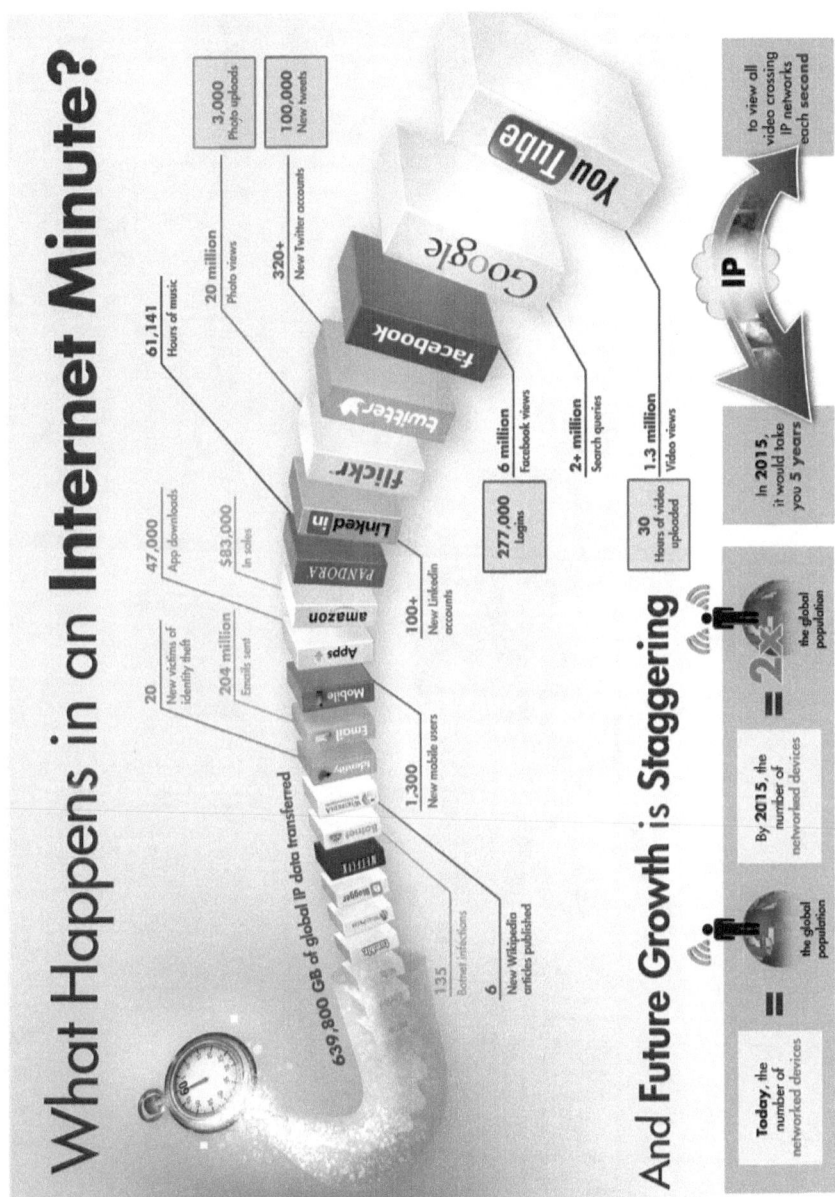

Figure 49 - Sample Project Communication Infographic[46]

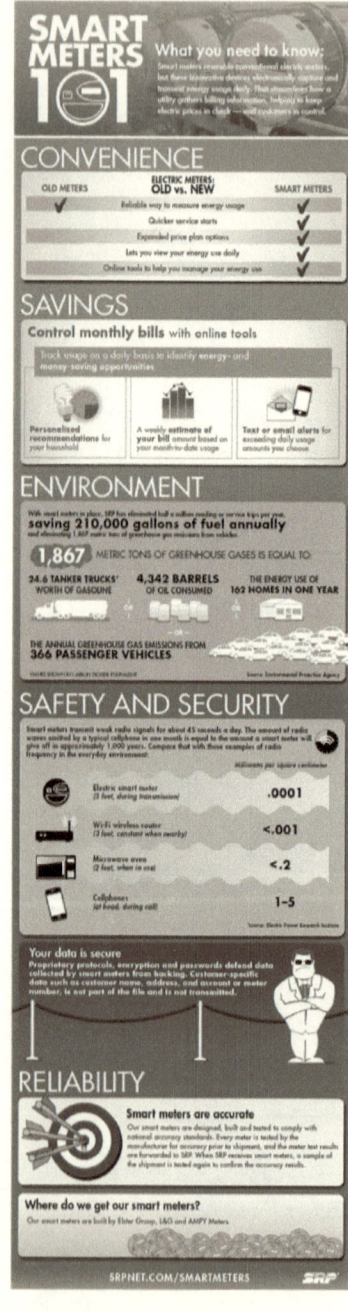

Figure 50 - Infographic-Based Project Milestone Plan[47]

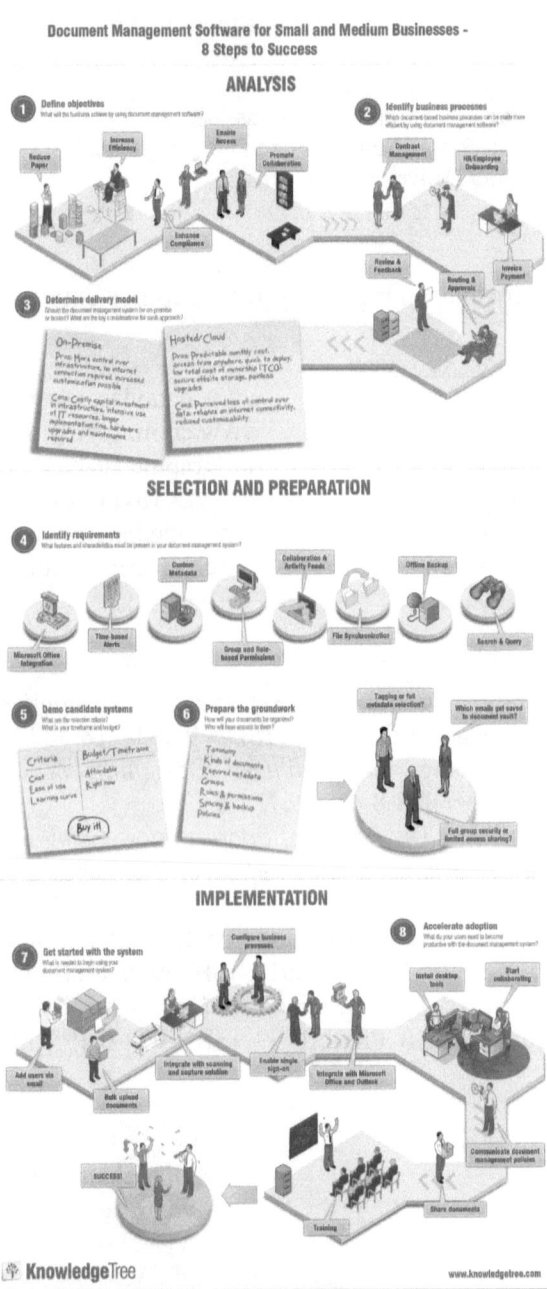

Using Infographics in Project Management Practice:

1. Project Status Reporting
2. Key Stakeholder Communications
3. Project Marketing Materials and Public Communications
4. Process and Deliverable Checklists

For additional information regarding Infographics concepts[xiv]:

General Information & Resources
The Data Visualization Catalogue: www.datavizcatalogue.com
Cool Infographics Blog: www.coolinfographics.com
Infographic Database: infographicdatabase.com
Visual Literacy Guide: bit.ly/IX1bvI (*case sensitive*)
Infographic (Wikipedia):   en.wikipedia.org/wiki/Infographic
Creative Commons Search Engine: search.creativecommons.org

Books
        Krum, Randy, *Cool Infographics: Effective Communication with Data Visualization and Design*, Wiley, 2013, ISBN 978-1-118-58230-5
        Shaoqiang, Wang, *Infographics: Designing & Visualizing Data*, Promopress, 2014, ISBN 978-8-415-96724-8
        Smiciklas, Mark, *The Power of Infographics: Using Pictures to Communicate and Connect with Your Audience*, Que Publishing, 2012, ISBN 978-0-789-74949-9
        Lankow, Jason, Ritchie, Josh and Crooks, Ross, *Infographics: The Power of Visual Storytelling*, Wiley, 2012, ISBN 978-1-118-31404-3
        Harris, Robert L., *Information Graphics: A Comprehensive Illustrated Reference*, Oxford University Press, 1999. ISBN 978-0-195-13532-9

Popular Software Tools
Piktochart™   www.piktochart.com
VennGage™   www.venngage.com
Visual.ly™   create.visual.ly
Gliffy™   www.gliffy.com

[xiv] See Legal Disclaimer (pg. iv)

Visual Project Collaboration

Project War Room

Whether they are called war rooms, situation rooms, command centers or mission control rooms, centralized and purpose-built project meeting spaces provide a dedicated location for project teams and stakeholders to co-locate and visually communicate the activities associated with the execution of critical projects. The idea of a war room is to physically gather an entire project team into a 'single location' in order to facilitate communication, problem solving, risk mitigation and status reporting. The single location can be physical, virtual or some combination of the two based on the specifics of the organization's business structure and/or resource model.

The establishment of a project management war room is a focused and deliberate organizational commitment. War rooms are designed to support administration of complex projects through the visualization of key project performance data specifically designed to facilitate informed decision-making and/or corrective action. War rooms are especially useful for collaborative activities such as breaking down complex project deliverables and processes into "workable" tasks or reviewing issues and risks, including the development of responses or mitigation plans.

War rooms also serve as a controlled source for communicating important project information that may include posting of change notices, requests for immediate actions/decisions or general status updates. These communications also typically include data visualizations of key performance metrics such as budget, schedule, issues, risks and overall project health. The main goal of any project war room is to communicate effectively enough so that anyone unfamiliar with the project should be able to grasp the status of the project rather quickly upon entering the room.

Modern day corporate war rooms are modeled after military command centers set up during World War II. Those wartime rooms focused on wall maps, table-sized charts, raw intelligence data and models representing force levels, location and movement. Based on the intelligence data gathered, the rooms were used to secretly conduct strategic and scenario planning sessions, along with executing tactical operations. The use of these rooms significantly aided military and political leaders by providing a centralized location for fact-based knowledge sharing and well-informed decision-making.

While not focused on winning an armed conflict (thankfully!), project management war rooms provide much of the same knowledge sharing and decision-making benefits of their military counterpart:

- Direct, as-needed, verbal communications between team members rather than a reliance on phone conversations, emails or the need for separate meetings
- Heightened sense of team commitment, togetherness and feeling of shared responsibility
- Complete focus on the effort and its end-goal rather than "business-as-usual" or daily operations
- A controlled, single-source hub of information for leaders, contributors, stakeholders and interested lay-people
- Increased awareness of performance or other important metrics

Studies show that creating a war room accelerates knowledge sharing, identification of task-level work, understanding of business processes and visualization of strategic opportunities.[48] They also add a spatial benefit by providing a dedicated work space for impromptu discussions, issue deliberations, data collection and analysis, and creative problem solving activities.[49] [50] A war room also eliminates the wasted time and energy spent scheduling meetings, securing meeting rooms and preserving meeting artifacts.

Figure 51 - Example of a Project War Room[51]

War Room Design and Maintenance Considerations:

1. Physical War Room Facilities
   a. Large main table with comfortable chairs
   b. Small semi-private work spaces
   c. Small collaboration or huddle spaces
   d. Appropriate high-tech tools
      • PCs/monitors, laptops, tablet devices, flat panel display(s), projection units/screen(s), digital camera(s), networking/ wireless connectivity, etc.
   e. Appropriate low-tech tools
      • Whiteboards, markers, easel pads, pencils/pens (including color), notebooks, sticky notes, stickers, sticky flags, office supplies, etc.
   f. Lots of wall space
      • Cork bulletin boards, magnet boards, foam boards, mounted white boards, erasable wall paint, tape, tacks, pins, removable adhesive, hanging strips, etc.
   g. Environmental
      • Kitchen items, coffee machine, a place for food, a small refrigerator for drinks, a snack basket, comfortable chairs, creativity "toys" and games, etc.

2. Design and Operation Best Practices
   a. Co-locate all project team members into the war room, even if some are virtual or remote
   b. As a team, come up with a set of "Rules for the War Room" and stick to them
   c. If possible, create a separate schedule/calendar for project team members so they are not distracted by other projects or daily operations
   d. Reserve work spaces for visiting or transient key project stakeholders that are not co-located with the rest of the project team
   e. Develop a method to reduce distractions by allowing the team to hang a "Do Not Disturb" sign when focused work or critical meetings are taking place
   f. Create a real estate map of the project war room to define what visual information will be displayed where:
      • Announcements and Key Communications
      • Rules of the War Room
      • Status Reports
      • Project Schedule
      • Project Budget
      • Issue/Risk Board
      • Design Diagrams, Process Maps, Wireframes, Storyboards, Photos, Drawings, etc.
      • Parking Lot Area (for out-of-scope or later phase consideration)
      • Blank Spaces for New Concepts/Discussions
   g. Provide plenty of snacks, healthy alternatives and beverages where possible
   h. Allow the project team to design and decorate the work space to match their personality and to encourage a sense of comfort and ownership
3. War Room Etiquette
   a. Keep visual displays up to date and meaningful
   b. Maintain a war room that is a "living," constantly changing space that encourages open discussion, healthy debate and cross-functional problem solving

    c. Do not remove or cover-up someone else's work in the display area(s) without first consulting with them

    d. Do not attempt to have private or confidential conversations in the war room

In a nutshell, the Project War Room is essentially a room-sized communication tool. Everything in the room is visible to anyone in the organization. Project team members, who work in the room for the duration of the project, call it home. They can also see and hear what everyone else in the room is working on, which creates a self-sustaining culture of accountability. Project stakeholders, who visit the room on a regular basis, can quickly get up to speed on progress, current status and any issues that may be facing the team. This allows them to engage and participate immediately, rather than waiting for a dedicated status meeting.

Figure 52 - Project War Room Example

Because the concept of leveraging project war rooms is not typical project management practice in most organizations, references to additional resources, web sites, books and/or available software are very limited. The reader is encouraged to consult internet search engines and other similar research materials when seeking additional information regarding this topic.

Using War Rooms in Project Management Practice:

1. Project Status Reporting
2. Key Stakeholder Communications
3. Project Marketing Materials and Public Communications
4. Project Team Management

Project "Science Fair"

In the traditional sense, science fairs are events, sometimes competitive in nature, where school-aged participants design and present visual-based information in the form of display boards, models, exhibits or reports regarding a particular scientific topic or research initiative. These fairs showcase student knowledge, stimulate creative problem solving and innovative thinking, and allow for friendly competition among schools or teams.

The notion of applying the "science fair" concept within project management practice is admittedly on the cutting edge for most in the profession. Their use, however, is not entirely unfamiliar. Project management offices (PMOs) and portfolio management leadership in large organizations have used project science fairs, also referred to as project expos or project forums, to showcase projects that have produced new products and/or services, along with projects that have made significant financial, process or operational impact on the organization. While creating an individual informational kiosk in a corporate common area is typical for sharing the results and benefits of a large, individual project effort, project science fairs are often leveraged when the goal is to showcase a number of key projects, programs or portfolios that have been successfully executed over a recent period of time.

These fairs serve as effective, informative, informal and fun internal marketing events where employees, at any level of the organization, can learn more about key project-based initiatives occurring within the organization. Additionally, project teams, stakeholders and sponsors can use the science fair concept as a way to showcase their contributions to project planning and execution activities throughout the year. Other benefits that the science fair concept brings to an organization include:

- Significantly increased awareness across the organization for project-based efforts and how they align with corporate strategies
- Increased visibility, recognition and expressions of appreciation for project team members
- Provide a sense of closure and celebration for the project team
- Demonstrate effectiveness of project-based management approaches
- Internal recruiting mechanism for people interested in working on future project teams

Figure 53 - Example of a Corporate Project "Science Fair"

Tips for Leveraging the Science Fair Concept in Project Management:

1. Determine Participation Method
   a. Application-Based Participation
      - Project teams apply for inclusion in the organization's annual showcase event and are either selected by event organizers or are voted in by fellow employees
   b. Selective or Portfolio-Based Participation
      - Projects are selected by the organization's executive or portfolio level management team to represent key project initiatives within each of the strategic or product portfolios
   c. Full Showcase Participation
      - All organizational project teams are invited to participate in the event
   d. Individual Participation
      - Single projects with significant organizational impact or benefit are showcased ad hoc to celebrate project completion, recognize noteworthy project benefit delivery (financial, societal, other) or to highlight other success factors important to the organization
2. Event Logistics
   a. Space Considerations
      - Individual or Small Events
        - A table or kiosk located in a common area like reception, the break room, employee lounge, etc.
      - Larger Events
        - Board room, large conference room, auditorium, etc.
   b. Technical Considerations
      - Power availability
      - Projections or display monitors
      - Networking/WiFi/Internet access

3. Exhibit Considerations
   a. Keep it simple and fun
   b. Cardboard project display boards
   c. Video or electronic presentations
   d. "Show and Tell" models or exhibits
   e. White papers or reports
   f. Candy or give-away items

Figure 54 - Photo from 3M "15% Time" Showcase Event[52]

* Because the idea of using a science fair or similar concept is not typical project management practice in most organizations, references to additional resources, web sites, books and/or available software are very limited. The reader is encouraged to consult internet search engines and other similar research materials when seeking additional information regarding this topic.

Using Project "Science Fairs" in Project Management Practice:

1. Internal Project Marketing/Awareness Campaign
2. Project Celebration and Recognition
3. Public or Stakeholder Communications

Visual Project Displays

Visual displays of project-related data are quite common in project management practice. Whether found in a common area, shared project team space or on a factory floor, these displays share information, encourage collaboration, increase project visibility, communicate status and make data easy to interpret and understand. Four of the most commonly used visualization approaches for project management include project display walls, project showcases/exhibitions, project flight status displays and 3D virtual project environments.

Project Display Walls

For organizations that cannot accommodate or justify the corporate real estate commitment required for a dedicated war room, space can usually be found on a long wall or shared workspace area. "Project walls" include much of the same data visualization artifacts used in project war rooms. Many project walls are centralized project status boards with dashboard-like project status metrics posted and available for viewing by anyone in the organization. Similar walls may be confined to the PMO or individual department that is sponsoring the project work.

Since the team is not co-located in a single room, status reviews and project meetings are typically conducted through what is known as a "wall walk." In a wall walk, the project team collectively reviews all new items posted to the wall, as well as any visual summaries of project status or performance metrics in order to determine next steps or actions to be taken in the next work cycle.

Important to remember when using project walls, is to position them in areas where they can easily be accessed by the project team without the need to be scheduled or reserved, can accommodate the entire team standing around the wall during discussions or wall walks, and will not disturb surrounding workers when impromptu meetings or full project team reviews are taking place.

The display wall concept, similar to how war rooms are utilized, focus project team member attention on the work flow, current status, performance metrics, issues and/or bottlenecks of the project. Likewise, the walls provide project stakeholders and other passers-by with quick, visual insight into the real-time status of the project and make project-specific details easy to understand by anyone, not just those that speak the tribal language of the project.

Figure 55 - Project Display Wall Example[53]

Similarly, a concept known as a "collaboration wall" allows project team members to post or hang their work on a shared wall workspace. This promotes awareness of who is working on what and encourages impromptu, collaborative discussions. Posting work to the wall essentially starts a conversation, invites constructive criticism and encourages creative idea building. Collaboration walls typically do not depict project management information, but are instead a tool used by project team members, project stakeholders and others as a sort of library of supporting information, ideas, prototypes, similar concepts and food for thought as the project is designed, planned and executed.

Project Showcase or Exhibition

Some projects have such an impact on the organization or society-at-large that they are deserving of special attention or recognition.   To facilitate this recognition, some organizations create an exhibition area to showcase these projects and their artifacts or deliverables. Rather than being actively used for the day-to-day management of a project effort, the showcase or exhibition is typically used post-project to highlight awards the project may have won, display products and/or services that the project recently delivered, or to convey other information the project team or their sponsors/stakeholders wish to share with the entire organization or the general public. These displays are usually either static, created as a stand-alone exhibit with a set duration, or event-based, created for a one-time publicity, marketing or celebratory event.

Figure 56 – Static Project Showcase Example

For static showcases or exhibitions, organizations typically create space in public, common or heavy traffic areas. The most frequently used static showcases include built-in wall displays similar to trophy cases or stand-alone kiosks that display information, and may include an interactive feature to engage the viewer in the exhibit.

In some larger organizations, or firms that are very product oriented, the use of company museums, innovation centers, product display areas, or visitor welcome areas are common examples of spaces that showcase some of the products and services produced by the firm or accolades the company's projects or products have been awarded.

Figure 57 - Project Exhibit Example[54]

Event-based project exhibitions, on the other hand, are essentially a combination of visual project walls, project showcases and project "science fairs." These events are usually carefully planned, choreographed and produced. In most circumstances, project exhibitions are either run by the organization's sales and marketing team or its research and development division. They also are typically held with an external audience in mind, rather than for internal promotion.

From a sales and marketing perspective, project exhibitions showcase recent project deliverables such as new products, services, features or functionality. The events serve both as a marketing vehicle to get the word out about the new offering(s) and as a sales vehicle to allow prospective buyers to touch and feel the new products and/or services that have resulted from the organizational project effort. They also give the project team an opportunity to solicit feedback on product usage and performance, as well as serving as a form of recognition for team members who were part of the project effort.

Figure 58 – Event-Based Project Exhibition Example[55]

Engr. Banji Babarinde enlightening guests at the Kaztec Engineering stand about the company's achievements and milestones recorded

Research and development based project and portfolio events, on the other hand, focus primarily on what is in the product development pipeline and provide a "taste of what's to come." These events showcase projects that are in a proposed state, in-flight or nearing completion. Essentially, R&D opens its doors to the general public or a targeted audience and holds an event to showcase the projects which will make up the products, services and offerings of the future.

These events are about knowledge and idea sharing, professional review and feedback, product management and potential target market discussions. The idea is to share just enough information to pique interest, while not giving away so much that market or competitive advantage would be lost.

Figure 59 – 3M Innovation Center in Dubai, UAE[56]

Figure 60 - DuPont Innovation Center in Moscow, Russia[57]

Project Flight Planning and Status Boards

The usage of aeronautical terminology and analogies are common in project management practice. Perhaps it is because modern-day project management takes its historical roots from the early defense and space programs of the 1940s and 1950s. A few of these aeronautic terms and analogies are visual in nature: Project Flight Plans, Project Flight Paths and Project Status Boards.

Project Flight Plans

Project flight plans are, in essence, a summary of the complete plan for the lifecycle of the project. They are critical for ensuring that all of the pre-flight (execution) checks have been completed, the required waypoint (milestone or deliverable) plans have been documented, the necessary crew (team) are assembled and ready, and that all of the plans have been reviewed and approved by the control tower (PMO or Executive Team).

Figure 61 - Flight Plans (Actual FAA Plan & Sample PMO Project Flight Plan Template)

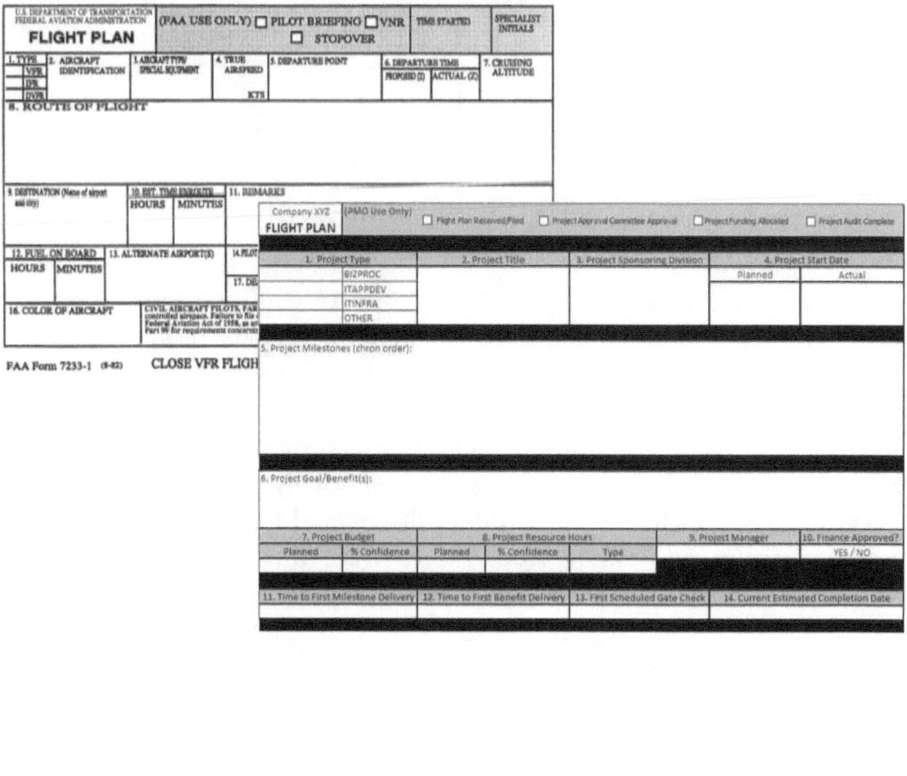

The project flight plan approach can also be extended to the concept of checklists. Checklists are an invaluable time saving tool for project managers. While typically not graphical in nature, when looking over a checklist, a user of the template can clearly see whether or not a task has been completed via "checked/not checked" visual capability.

Figure 62 - Project Management Process Checklist Example 1

Initiation	Planning
Project Management Tasks	**Project Management Tasks**
○ Project Kick-Off Meeting with Sponsor & SME Team	○ Project Kick-Off Meeting with Project Team
○ Complete Project Initiation Workbook	○ Detailed Business Requirements Analysis
○ Draft Project Scope/High-Level Requirements/Charter	○ Work Breakdown Structure/Task Sheet
○ Submit Project Cost Planning Worksheet	○ Build Project Schedule
○ Draft Project Request for Approval Presentation	○ Identify Project Risks and Mitigation Plans
○ Draft Project Communications Plan	○ Identify Project Issues, Target Resolution Date and Owners
○	○ Populate Project Financial Tracking Workbook
○	○ Create Project EV/Milestone Worksheet
○	○ Schedule Project Planning Working Sessions
○	○
○	○
○	○
○	○
○	○
Documentation Required	**Documentation Required**
○ Project Initiation Workbook	○ Project Issues Logged
○ Project Charter / Scope Document	○ Project Risks Logged
○ Project Cost Planning Worksheet	○ Work Breakdown Structure Document
○ Business Case/CBA	○ MS Project Task Plan/Schedule
○ Project Team Roster & RACI	○ High-Level Budget/Forecast/Actuals in Innotas
○ Project Request for Approval Presentation	○ Project Financial Tracking Workbook
○ Project Communications Plan Document	○ Project Earned Value/Milestone Worksheet
○	○ Meeting Agendas/Minutes/Notes
○	○
○	○
Project Management Checkpoints	**Project Management Checkpoints**
○	○ Project Leadership Team Approval
○	○
○	○
Technical Checkpoints	**Technical Checkpoints**
○ Technology Architecture Review #1	○ Technology Architecture Review #2
○	○
○	○

In the early 2000s, Atul Gawande, a surgeon and author, was researching innovative new methods to prevent common medical errors. In his research, he stumbled across simple checklists produced by the United States Air Force that enable pilots to fly incredibly sophisticated modern aircraft. Pilots know how to fly airplanes; it's what they are trained to do. But flying airplanes requires knowledge of very complex processes, and a single mistake in any part of the process would have disastrous consequences. The military discovered that, through the use of checklists, pilot and flight crew safety were drastically improved by consulting various lists of important "must do" items before, during and after flight. Similarly, in his book, "The Checklist Manifesto[58]," Gawande details how the use of simple checklists that remind doctors to follow proper hand washing protocol prior to surgery led to a dramatic reduction in post-surgical patient infection rates.

Pilots and surgeons (and project managers) are intuitively expected to know complex processes, tools and procedures as part of their professional craft. Added to that complexity is the stressful work environment that pilots and surgeons (and project managers) are expected to operate. The use of checklists cuts through this complexity and quiets the noise of stress by serving as thoughtful reminders of tasks that must be completed in order to accomplish a specific goal: flight, surgery, project or otherwise.

Figure 63 - Project Management Process Checklist Example 2

Execution		Closing	
Project Management Tasks		**Project Management Tasks**	
○	Schedule Project Execution SCRUM Meetings	○	Create Project Punchlist Tracking Worksheet
○	Schedule Project Leadership Team Review Meetings	○	Confirm Project Tasks Complete/Closed
○	Facilitate Project Team SCRUM Meetings	○	Final Balance Project Financial Tracking Documentation
○	Facilitate Project Leadership Team Meetings	○	Close Project Risks
○	Project Status Reporting	○	Close Project Issues
○	Update Project Task Plan/Schedule	○	Complete Project EV/Milestone Worksheet
○	Track Project Spending and Hour Consumption Rate	○	Document Lessons Learned
○	Update EV/Milestone Worksheet	○	Project Recognition
○	Identify Project Issues, Target Resolution Date and Owners	○	Project Files/Artifacts to Storage
○	Identify Project Risks and Mitigation Plans	○	
○	Draft Project Test Plans	○	
○	Conduct SIT/UAT Testing	○	
○	Manage Change Control	○	
○	Review Communications Plan (Go-Live Communications)	○	
○		○	
○		○	
Documentation Required		**Documentation Required**	
○	Project Status Updates	○	Project Closing Punchlist Tracking Worksheet
○	Project Issues Logged	○	Project Financial Tracking Workbook
○	Project Risks Logged	○	MS Project Task Plan/Schedule
○	Update MS Project Task Plan/Schedule	○	Project Closing Artifact Document
○	Communications Plan / Go-Live Communications	○	Project Closing Sign-Off Sheet
○	Meeting Agendas/Minutes/Notes	○	Lessons Learned Document
○	Project Financial Tracking Workbook	○	
○	Project Earned Value/Milestone Worksheet	○	
○	Project Test Plan Documentation	○	
○		○	
○		○	
Project Management Checkpoints		**Project Management Checkpoints**	
○	Project Team Go/No-Go Approval	○	Project Leadership Team Project Closing Approval
○	Project Leadership Team Go/No-Go Approval	○	
○		○	
○		○	
Technical Checkpoints		**Technical Checkpoints**	
○	Technology Architecture Validation	○	Technology Architecture Sign-Off
○		○	
○		○	

Project Flight Paths

Project teams are often viewed as instruments of organizational change. While it is unfair to place such a burden on them, the logic is understandable. By definition, project teams are tasked with implementing something new to the organization. In this process of adding a new "thing," often times an existing "thing" is changed or eliminated.   This often causes organizational reactions that can be positive, neutral and/or negative.

The anticipation of, and strategic responses for, these reactions is known as organizational change management, and is a field of study and profession all its own.   One of the most common tools used in organizational change management is the flight path scenario that mimics an airplane's flight path from one location (current state), through a series of maneuvers (changes) and eventually resulting in a safe arrival at the destination (future desired state).

The flight path analogy sets the framework for the lifecycle of the planned organizational change. It provides stakeholders involved in the change with a visual depiction of the entire change journey so they know what to expect and when. It also clearly states the final destination so that people can begin to come to terms with the change on a more personal level.

Figure 64 - Typical Flight Path Steps

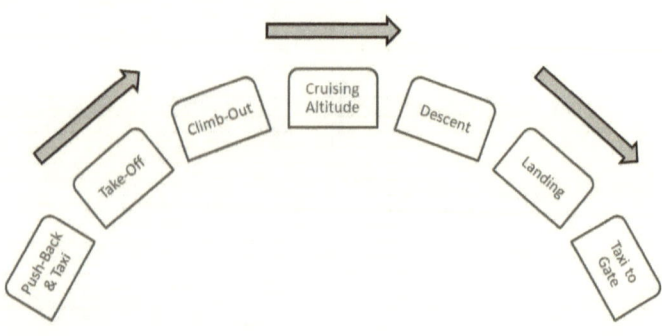

Figure 65 - Flight Path Aligned to Project Management Processes

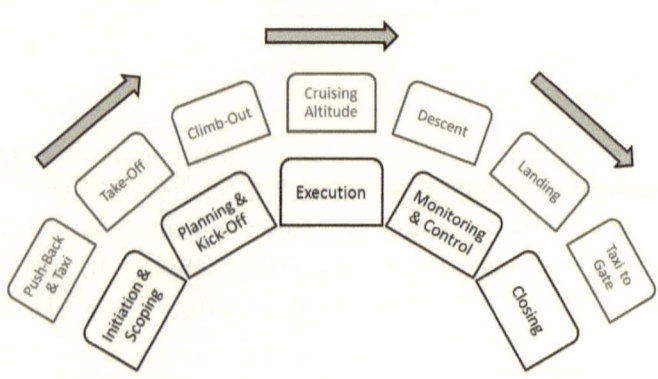

Figure 66 - Example of Actual Project Usage of the Flight Path Concept

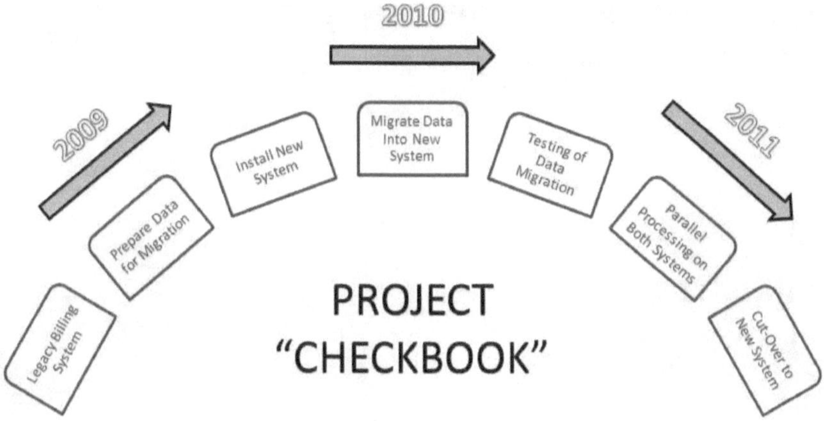

Project Airport Status Boards

Project status boards are simple, at-a-glance visual representations of real-time project status across a number of different projects or across multiple sub-teams/work streams on a single project. Status boards range from the very simple to the very sophisticated. Simple boards are often represented on a magnetic white board with project names listed and color-coded magnets utilized to signify status, or via a simple color printed spreadsheet (see figure 67).

Figure 67 - Project Status Board – Simple

PROJECTS	Overall Status	Budget Status	Schedule Status	Scope Status	Status Notes	Planned Finish	Estimated Finish
Project A	GREEN	GREEN	GREEN	GREEN	On Track	12/31/2013	12/23/2013
Project B	YELLOW	YELLOW	GREEN	GREEN	Over Budget	12/31/2013	12/31/2013
Project C	GREEN	GREEN	GREEN	YELLOW	Scope Change Pending	4/30/2014	2/28/2014
Project D	RED	YELLOW	RED	YELLOW	Cancelled	6/30/2014	Cancelled
Project E	YELLOW	GREEN	YELLOW	GREEN	Delayed	6/30/2014	7/31/2014

Electronic project status boards have been developed in the last few years and are becoming more and more affordable as the technology costs decrease and product maturity increases. While in use across multiple industry types, much of the development around electronic status boards are found in software development environments. Figure 68 represents an advanced online status board in use at Microsoft® while Figure 69 represents a very sophisticated status board displayed on two flat panel monitors at app/software development firm, Panic.[59]

Figure 68 - Project Status Board – Advanced[60]

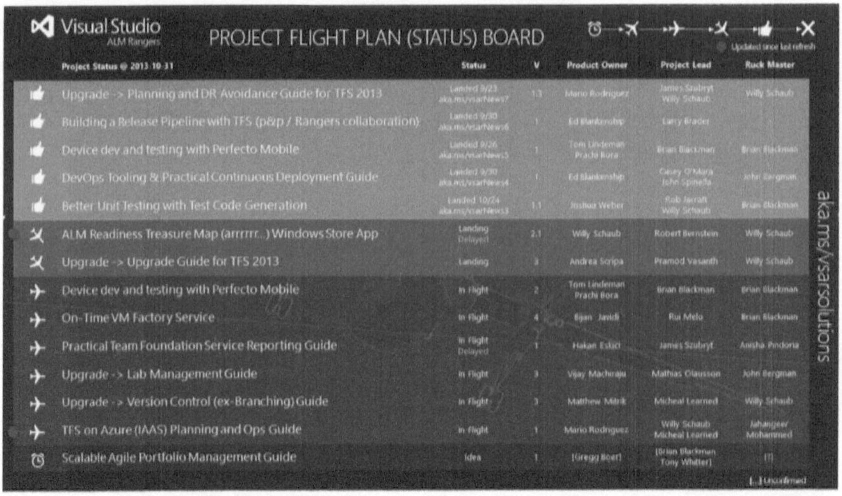

Figure 69 - Project Status Board Example - Sophisticated[61]

3D Project Environments

    The utilization of 3D environments in project management practice is a very recent development and its usage is typically defined by the industry in which the projects are undertaken. For example, new product development projects that rely on rapid prototyping are eagerly leveraging new developments in 3D printing technology. Once limited only to concept modelers, artists and design teams, proposed product designs can be transformed from a 2D image on a computer monitor to a 3D physical object that can be "printed" in a matter of hours. As 3D printers continue to become more and more mainstream (and affordable), usage of the technology for project tasks such as prototyping, modeling, testing and usability will become a reality within even the smallest product development shops.

For organizations that focus more on marketing, customer experience and product placement projects, complete 3D store layouts and virtual shopping aisles are being developed. For example, consumer packaged goods firm, Kimberly-Clark, launched their "Innovation Design Studio" in 2007, which uses a proprietary virtual reality system to simulate product placement on various levels of grocery store aisle shelves. Product development and customer experience teams conduct focus group sessions and leverage high-tech eye tracking technology, testing various product placement strategies by soliciting direct feedback and recording the reactions and engagement of the "shopper."

3D virtual reality environments have also started to show up on mobile apps. The reader is encouraged to download and view the app for retail pharmacy chain CVS on either iOS™ or Android™ mobile platforms for an excellent example of a "virtual pharmacy." Similarly, the online virtual world known as SecondLife® once enjoyed a significant following in the business and professional communities. Launched in 2003, usage has since waned, but there are still a significant number of business enterprises, test labs and customer experience simulations available for further study.

Finally, with an increasing number of project team members participating virtually from locations all across the globe, the creation of temporary virtual project "war rooms" have also been on the increase. These electronic communities often include video conferencing technology, virtual white boards, screen sharing, access to a shared document repository, electronic "bulletin boards" for information sharing and other modules designed to allow a widely dispersed project team to communicate and collaborate "virtually."

Using Visual Project Displays in Project Management Practice:

1.   Project Team, Stakeholder and/or Public Communications
2.   Change Management Visualization
3.   Project Planning and Task Validation
4.   Portfolio Planning and Sequencing

For additional information regarding Visual Project Display concepts[xv]:

Books

Tufte, Edward, *The Visual Display of Quantitative Information*, Graphics Press, 2001, ISBN 978-0-961-39214-7

Sibbet, David, *Visual Meetings: How Graphics, Sticky Notes and Idea Mapping Can Transform Group Productivity*, Wiley, 2010, ISBN 978-0-470-60178-5

Lester, Paul Martin, *Visual Communication: Images with Messages*, Cengage Learning, 2013, ISBN 978-1-133-30864-5

Gawande, Atul, *The Checklist Manifesto: How to Get Things Right*, Metropolitan Books, 2009, ISBN 978-0-805-09174-8

Hodge, Elizabeth, Collins, Sharon and Giordano, Tracy, *The Virtual Worlds Handbook: How to Use SecondLife® and Other 3D Virtual Environments*, Jones & Bartlett Learning, 2009, ISBN 978-0-763-77747-0

[xv] See Legal Disclaimer (pg. iv)

Project Social Media

Without question, social media and social networking have been a dominant force in the last decade. What started with simple online tools to manage personal relationships has exploded into massive virtual communities and networks designed to exchange data, information and ideas. They have become an entirely new form of communication, available to anyone with a connection to the internet. In fact, according to research done by Nielsen, internet users spend more time on social media sites than any other type of site and that the percentage of total time spent on social media increases exponentially every year.[62]

Key to the social media wave has been the creation and sharing of user-generated content. This new concept has transferred the power of information distribution away from traditional sources such as news outlets and publishing conglomerations, and into the hands and minds of individual people. Its reach and influence have increased drastically beyond simple social status sharing and have become sources of real-time news, e-commerce business platforms and often times require the use of social media management tools that help integrate multiple social media accounts under one master umbrella.

Because social media platforms are so ubiquitous, it is easy to assume that most people understand all of the technologies classified as social media. Social media platforms include internet forums, weblogs (blogs), wikis, social networks, pod/vid casting, photo/video sharing, social bookmarking, e-magazines/newspapers, rating sites and opinion or comment sites. (see Figure 70)

Figure 70 - The Social Media Spectrum[63]

Because the growth of social media has extended beyond simple personal usage and is now acceptable (at least partially) for use within the business enterprise, the search for the effective and efficient application of these new tools is underway in most organizations. From a project management perspective, the use of these new collaboration and communication tools have the potential to boost productivity, improve learning opportunities, shrink gaps between remote user/sites and potentially even reduce cost. These possible gains, however, also come with inherent risks in the form of data security and privacy issues, a lack of productive work focus and a decline in physical interpersonal relationships. These risks need to be actively considered by project management practitioners as participation on certain social media platforms may violate organizational security policies and/or unintentionally expose confidential or protected company information to the public domain.

So how can the use of social media be leveraged to improve project management collaboration and communication? In the next few pages, some of the most popular social media technologies will be briefly explored, along with possible project management-specific uses that can be aligned with those technologies.

Facebook® (facebook.com)
Facebook is an online social networking platform where users create a user profile, add other users as "friends", exchange messages, post status updates and photos, share videos and receive notifications when others update their profiles. Facebook is the largest social network in the world with 1.3 billion active users as of June 2014.

While Facebook is the dominant player in social media, its usage in project management practice is rather limited. There are, however, a number of specific uses that project managers may find to be beneficial in using Facebook:

1. Connections with other project management professionals for knowledge sharing and networking
2. Educational and professional development activity with leading providers, associations and thought leaders
3. Creation of special project "pages" for posting task completion status, project document artifacts and other project-related information that has been approved for public consumption.

Twitter® (twitter.com)

Twitter is an online social networking service with an estimated 284 million active users worldwide that enables users to send and read short 140-character messages called "tweets". Twitter has often been referred to as a "river of information," with a constant flow of tweets that never stops. Using this same analogy, users of Twitter are said to periodically wade into this fictional river, consuming information as it flows past.

Because this flow of information can be overwhelming, there are a few tools available that focus the consumption of the rapidly changing stream: Hashtags, Lists and Advanced Searches. A "hashtag," noted by the symbol #, is simply a keyword that identifies the subject matter of the tweet. For project managers, common hashtags include: #pmot (for project management on twitter), #projectmanager, #pmp, #project and, following the release of this work, #visualpm. Because the creation and use of hashtags are open to users, some project management teams have created project-specific hashtags to communicate among themselves such as: #AcmeProjectZeus. Note that tweets and hashtags are public and caution should be used when posting project-related information.

Project teams can also create public or private lists of Twitter users. Many project managers maintain accounts on Twitter and post valuable information related to the profession. Creating a list of these users and following their tweets can be a valuable source of professional development. Lists can be public or private. While most tweets are public, the aggregation of tweets among members of private lists is only available to the members of that list. Project teams that wish to communicate on Twitter can form a private list limited only to project team members, stakeholders, etc. Only one-to-one tweets, known as Direct Messages, are considered truly private on Twitter.

Finally, using the 'Advanced Search' feature of Twitter, users can search content using more advanced conditions such as words, people, places, dates and emotion-based search criteria. The reader is encouraged to consult the help function on Twitter.com for more information on how to effectively and efficiently use the Twitter social media platform.

Virtual Communities

Project teams, especially geographically diverse teams, can establish an online community using any number of available technical platforms. These communities allow project teams to share announcements, create team-based calendars of meetings, vacations or key milestones, create team or topic-specific web pages, establish a document repository and participate in forum-like conversations. Virtual community sites allow project teams to feel more like a cohesive team with the additional benefit of having a "one-stop shop" for all project-related information and documentation.

Examples of virtual community platforms include:
1. Google+™ (plus.google.com)
2. Yammer™ (yammer.com)
3. Microsoft SharePoint™ (products.office.com/sharepoint/)

Blogging and Wiki Pages

Perhaps one of the original social media categories to be utilized by the project management community, web logs, better known simply as blogs, are in wide use both publically on the internet and privately on thousands of corporate intranets around the world. Blogs can be used to share information, post status reports or other announcements, facilitate discussions via comments, capture and store knowledge, log change requests and tag blog entries for easy information categorization.

Wiki pages are similar to blogs but add the feature of interactivity and on-the-fly editing capability. Once a wiki page is created, anyone with permissions to do so can add to or edit the page. Some project management teams use this functionality like a team diary, where entries on status, progress and key information are stored and then appended to daily, providing a living history of the conversation. Other teams use wiki pages to document project scope and requirements documentation, as any changes are automatically logged, capturing the editor and the date/time stamp when the change occurred. Still other teams simply use wiki pages to post and exchange information and facilitate conversations.

Examples of blog and wiki page creation include:
1. Blogger™ (blogger.com)
2. WordPress® (wordpress.org and wordpress.com)
3. SquareSpace® (squarespace.com)
4. WikiSpaces® (wikispaces.com)
5. TWiki® (twiki.org)

Podcasting/Vidcasting/YouTube™

These technologies are especially useful for geographically dispersed teams. Podcasting is the recording of a voice communication and sharing it online. Podcasts can either be broadcast to the public or made private behind a subscription-based authentication system. Numerous project management teams have taken to dictating project status reports, recording project team meetings for later playback or distribution to non-attendees, as well as delivering project training via podcast. As long as the project team members have appropriate podcast play-back tools, the podcasts can be made available to anyone.

Vidcasting is essentially the same as podcasting, except the media is video-based. This becomes an even more valuable tool if the project team has adopted a visual project management approach. Vidcasting technology ranges from traditional video recording, to screen sharing overlaid with the video, and beyond to multi-paned/multi-media displays shared with the video presentation. While YouTube is the most popular upload repository and search site for video productions on the internet, vidcasts, or other video-based media, can be stored anywhere and similar sites exist elsewhere on the internet. Similar to podcasting, consumers of the video media simply need to have appropriate software to view the productions and both public and private options exist.

Additional Social Media Options for Project Managers:
1. Pinterest® (pinterest.com)
    a. A relatively new option for project management teams, Pinterest is a social media platform that offers visual collection, sharing and search tools. Users create and share collections of visual bookmarks, known as boards. Boards are created when a user selects a photo, graphic, website, etc. and pins it to a categorized board. While mostly used to share recipes and interior decorating photos, savvy project managers use the site to share visual project media like dashboards, infographics and other data visualizations.
2. Document Sharing Sites
    a. While usage of document sharing sites has been traditionally limited by organizational information security policies, a number of sites have tightened up their security measures and offer corporate versions of their services. Document sharing sites like Dropbox™ (dropbox.com), Prezi™ (prezi.com), SlideShare™ (slideshare.net) and others can serve as a centralized,

cloud-based location for project documentation and presentations, project management training modules and other project document archives.

3. Professional Networking Sites

   a. Sites such as LinkedIn® (linkedin.com) or even project management specific sites like pmi.org, projectmanagement.com, projectconnections.com and others provide professional development, networking and self-promotion opportunities. While not typically used on a project-level basis, these sites prove especially valuable when searching for potential project team candidates, consultants or other needed project resources.

4. Bookmarking Sites

   a. Using social bookmarking sites like Evernote™ (evernote.com) and Reddit™ (reddit.com) allow project team members to tag pages, tweets, posts, blogs and other web-based locations for future reference.

Social media is an extraordinary opportunity to improve team communication and collaboration at all levels. That collaboration should be fun, easy to use and provide a platform that is open to idea sharing, information and knowledge exchange, and improving the effectiveness and consistency of project communications. After all, it is well known that most project-related problems result from communication issues on some level.

Most project team members and stakeholders are likely already quite comfortable, perhaps even proficient, with social media technology. Additionally, usage of social media has rapidly eroded the barrier between personal and professional interactions. With the myriad of tools that have been developed for almost every conceivable communication and collaboration use, taking the leap into social media for project management should be a quick and relatively simple transition for the project team to make.

When exploring potential social media platforms or concepts to use in project management practice, there are a number of recommended considerations to review before implementing any solution:

1. What types of information does the team need to communicate, including the frequency and delivery method?
2. How geographically diverse is the project team?
3. How sensitive is the information being shared?
4. Is the information intended to be delivered in a push or pull communication method?
5. What social media platforms and technologies does the project team already use and are comfortable with using?
6. What non-project benefits can be realized using social media tools? (networking, professional development, skill enhancement, etc.)

*** As always, the reader is strongly encouraged to consult first with their organizational or independent IT and/or information security professionals before making social media usage decisions, to ensure that confidential and proprietary project or organizational information is properly protected.*

> Using Social Media in Project Management Practice:
>
> 1. Project and Stakeholder Communications
> 2. Project Document Management
> 3. Project Team Professional Development

For additional information regarding Social Media concepts[xvi]:

Books
  Harrin, Elizabeth, *Social Media for Project Managers*, Project Management Institute, 2010, ISBN 978-1-935-58911-2
  Kawasaki, Guy and Fitzpatrick, Peg, *The Art of Social Media: Power Tips for Power Users*, Portfolio Hardcover, 2014, ISBN 978-1-591-84807-3

[xvi] See Legal Disclaimer (pg. iv)

Gamification in Project Management

Gamification is the application of game thinking and dynamics within non-game contexts, such as business operations, by engaging employees (players) to participate in solving business problems and completing work tasks in a fun, fulfilling and learning-based environment. While gamification has a "flavor-of-the-month" buzz around it today, and is subject to traditional business hype cycles, it is becoming an increasingly popular trend within business operations management and one that is being actively explored for possible use in project management practice. The statistics don't lie:

- The Association for Project Management conducted a study in 2012 which found that 3 billion hours world-wide are spent each week by people who are participating in some form of gaming.[64]
- A similar study conducted by Jane Gonigal in her book, "*Reality Is Broken*," found that, in the United States alone, there are 183 million active gamers.[65]
- According to research conducted by M2 Research, the gamification industry will grow from approximately $500 million in the United States in 2013 to an estimated $2.8 billion by the end of 2016[66]

The reason behind these impressive statistics, quite simply, is because people love to play games. Games provide a sense of personal accomplishment along with the sense of community that comes from being part of a team. Games also trigger natural instincts for competition and the positive emotions that come with the excitement that the potential for winning provides.

Gamification, while a relatively new term, traces its conceptual roots back to the first airline frequent flyer rewards programs. Established by airline marketing teams to increase brand loyalty, these programs used an accumulated point or miles-based system of award levels, which allowed participants to gain access to awards, perks, recognition and financial benefits not available to non-participants. In fact, one of the main findings from these early game-based systems was that the level of effectiveness of a program was greatly increased when the points or rewards had tangible economic value to participants. These programs proved that gamification can trigger basic, subliminal human needs and desires that include status and achievement.

In general, modern-day business usage of gamification seeks to increase employee engagement in daily or project-based work tasks by granting rewards and/or recognition via the use of points, achievement levels and/or accomplishment badges. The rewards are granted on any number of factors such as on-time (or early) task completion, accomplishment of more tasks than planned within a certain time-box, consecutive number of bug-free software code releases or reductions in defect rates. Gamification essentially helps to keep workers motivated and inspires them to achieve the best end results possible.

Figure 71 - Sample Gamification User Profile[67]

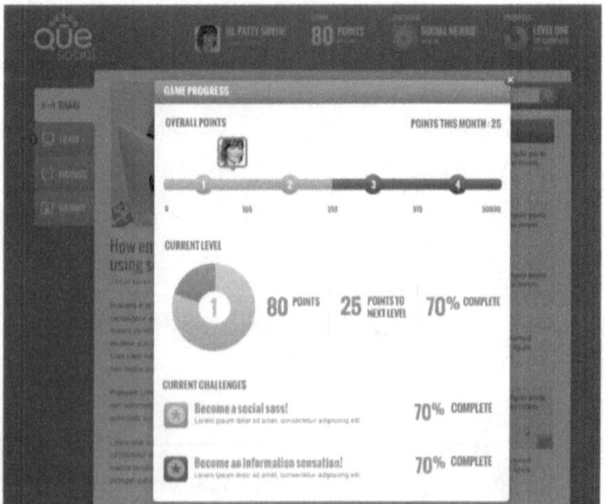

The collection of points and badges, or progressions through various game levels, is tracked on scoreboards or leaderboards, showing participants how they compare with their peers. Making the rewards for accomplishing tasks visible to other participants, or publically displaying leaderboards, encourage individuals and teams to compete, as the natural competitive nature of human beings provides a strong bias for action and increased performance.

Figure 72 - Sample Gamification Leaderboard[68]

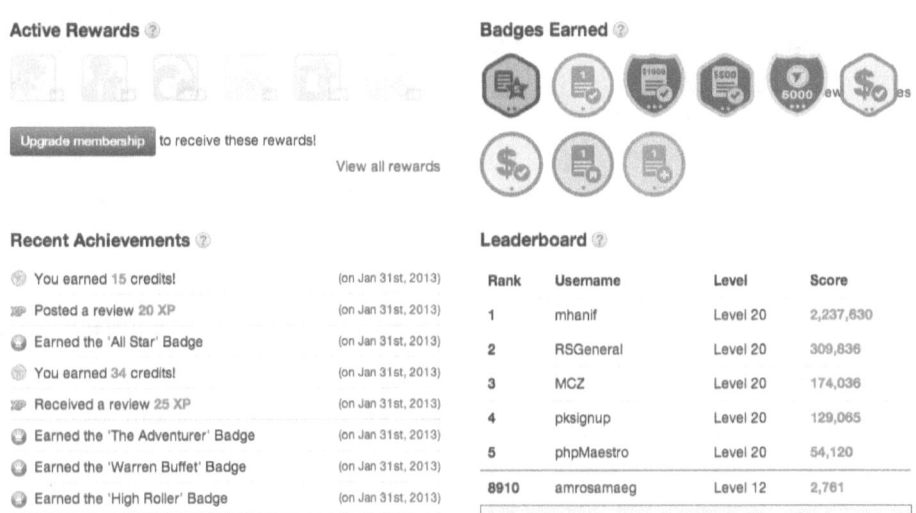

While competitive elements already exist in traditional work environments, adding the new wrinkle that gamification introduces can have both positive and negative results. Positive effects of the competitive nature via gamification include increased engagement, enhanced motivation, stronger collaboration and heightened performance within teams. Achieving these positive results, however, requires a transparent and consistent process of allocating rewards, tracking progress, providing feedback on results and a tiered system that effectively motivates people at every level to sustain engagement across the entire population of participants.

Caution is advised, however, to remain aware of the potential negative effects that may result from gamification, such as driving unintended "win at all costs" or dishonest behaviors. Badly designed or conducted gamification programs can lead to participant isolation, tension among competing teams, feelings of injustice and a lack of motivation for individuals or teams that rank in the lower half of the game's leaderboard. Another potential negative effect associated with gamification is if the game never ends. Long running or never-ending games reduce participation and eventually "poison the well" for future game-based activities.

So how is the gamification phenomenon applicable to project management practice? Projects and games share many common traits. Projects are managed by setting goals, breaking down the work needed to achieve the goals, defining roles needed to complete the work and establishing a set of metrics that are tracked following a defined lifecycle with milestones that show progress toward the end goal. In similar fashion, games also set goals for success, assign roles, establish rules, tasks and processes, encourage creative problem solving, reward success and progress, and follow a defined lifecycle that ultimately leads to the achievement of the goal, also known as winning the game.

Successful project managers understand that equally successful project results come about by actively engaging and motivating project team members. And since the use of gamification concepts are designed to improve engagement and motivation, it makes sense to attempt to combine the two and look for any enhanced benefits that can potentially be leveraged. Ultimately, the use of gamification in project management practice is to inspire team members to utilize a prescribed process, meet deadlines on a timely basis and improve upon project productivity and delivery metrics. Additionally, the use of gamification for project activities can also provide beneficial increases in key organizational and cultural attributes such as:

1. Fun, engaging and exciting work climate
2. Creativity and problem solving skills
3. Team cohesiveness
4. Individual and team productivity
5. Individual morale and retention
6. Quality of work product

Before embarking on a gamification journey, project managers should ensure they understand and document the specific long and short-term goals that the "gamified" process is intended to achieve. Applying gamification techniques without an end goal in mind is a recipe for failure.

Common project management-specific goals that lend themselves to gamification approaches include:

1. Maintaining high quality work by tracking defect rates, items returned from testing, etc.
2. Maintaining on-schedule project task delivery
3. Keeping up with required project administrative tasks like time recording, status reporting, issue logging, etc.
4. Improving accuracy of task estimation by comparing estimated effort to actuals
5. Cost reduction opportunities by developing creative solutions that reduce original estimates

Beyond point-based or achievement-based games, gamification also includes simulation. Simulations provide significant impact to all organizational teams whether they are project-based, process-based or technical. Simulations involve putting people into realistic, simulated environments that allow them to experience complex situations or best practices, while creating deeper understanding of available choices, potential risks and/or benefits, and expected results versus intended consequences. In fact, training-based simulations are perhaps the most mature example of the use of gamification in project management practice, having been available for a number of years. Possibly the largest benefit that simulations bring, similar to the more reward-based gamification approaches, is that they promote close team collaboration and communication.

Simulations are typically classroom-based scenario games that portray projects in various stages which face specific issues, risks, challenges and/or barriers to successful project delivery. The simulation allows participants to work together as a project team to practice collaboration, communication and problem solving around the various obstacles presented in the scenario.

In some simulations, players are guided through the same situational scenario numerous times, but deploying different approaches or methodologies in each round, such as: applying current organizational processes, then industry best practice processes are used and finally, innovative new approaches are tested. These repetitive scenarios allow the teams to learn the pros and cons of each approach as they relate to common problem sets. Simulations are essentially "live-fire" feedback sessions where the participants capture lessons learned as the impact and result of each potential decision is made.

Figure 73 - SimulTrain®10 Project Management Simulation Software Screenshot[69]

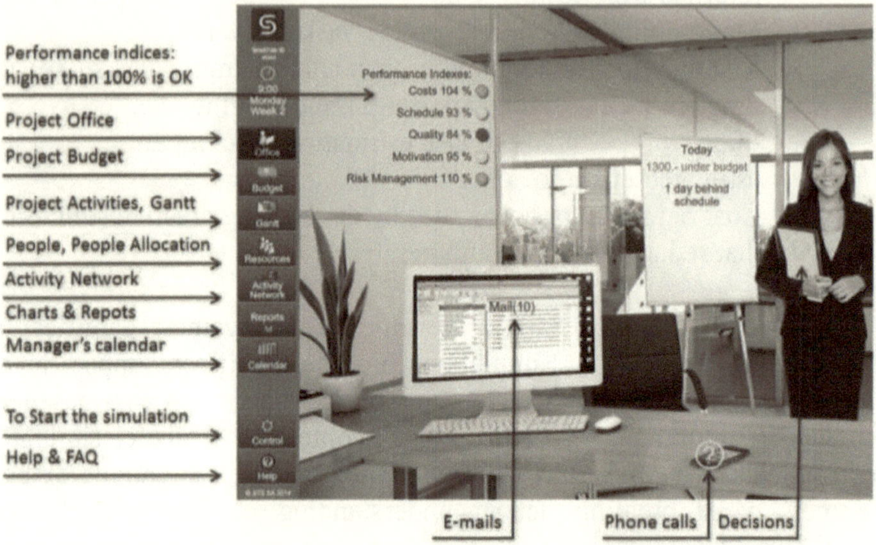

Beyond project management methodology or process training, the concept of simulation is completely applicable to scenarios generated from actual projects as well. When projects encounter thorny issues or risks, simulations can be leveraged to test certain risk mitigation options or issue resolution approaches. Simulations can also be used to provide the project team with better understanding of product usage or business process outcomes.

A number of consultancy-based and online project simulations are now available in the marketplace that facilitates design, execution and data gathering from the simulation sessions. These offerings range from project management skill building to realistic training environments for emergency scenarios. Because the concept of gamification is becoming more readily adopted, some larger software platforms like Oracle's customer relationship management solution known as Salesforce® is now offered with a gamification module built-in.

Using Gamification and Simulation in Project Management Practice:

1. Project Team Collaboration
2. Project Team Morale Improvement
3. Project Team Process Training
4. Risk/Issue Mitigation Planning and Testing

For additional information regarding Gamification concepts[xvii]:

General Information & Resources
Gamification (Wikipedia):   en.wikipedia.com/wiki/Gamification
Gamification.org: badgeville.com/wiki
SimStudios   simstudios.com
Dashboard Simulations: dashboardsimulations.com

Books
Gray, Dave and Brown, Sunni, *Gamestorming: A Playbook for Innovators, Rulebreakers and Changemakers*, O'Reilly Media, 2010, ISBN 978-0-596-80417-6

Kumar, Janaki and Herger, Mario, *Gamification At Work: Designing Engaging Business Software*, Interaction-Design.org, 2013, ISBN 978-8-792-96407-6

Burke, Brian, *Gamify: How Gamification Motivates People to Do Extraordinary Things*, Bibliomotion, 2014, ISBN 978-1-937-13485-3

Shtub, Avraham, *Project Management Simulation with Project Team Builder (PTB)*, Springer, 2012, ISBN 978-1-441-96462-5

Popular Software Tools and Online Vendors
Bunchball   www.bunchball.com/gamification
Badgeville   www.badgeville.com
SimulTrain®   www.sts.ch/en/products/simulation/simultrain
SimProject®   www.simulationpoweredlearning.com
Sandbox Model   www.sandboxmodel.com

[xvii] See Legal Disclaimer (pg. iv)

Epilogue

FACT: Project management is an extremely "data rich" business activity. At any given time, project management professionals are capturing, manipulating, transforming and communicating hundreds of individual data points. These data points include labor estimates, capital and operational expenses, task lists, performance metrics, calendars, cost-benefit analysis worksheets, risk profiles, trending data and a seemingly countless number of project documentation artifacts.

As the speed of business continues to increase, and as focus on an ever growing number of data points is needed to keep business and project execution in control, new and innovative tools and techniques are required to help busy executives make efficient and effective decisions on where to invest money and resources. Visualization of data and complex processes has proven valuable in serving those needs.

A project manager's world is already full of data visualizations, designed to transform complex and voluminous data into simple, effective communication tools. Traditional visualizations such as Gantt charts, work breakdown structures, Kanban boards, process diagrams, project team calendars, project stakeholder organization charts, and the like are beneficial in their own way, but they don't tell the collective story of overall project status and/or performance.

Complicating the matter, busy executive sponsors and key project stakeholders no longer have the luxury of time for lengthy project status reports or weekly status briefing meetings. Decisions must be made in the moment, with whatever facts are available. Because of this, traditional project management disciplines that leverage process and document heavy approaches are rapidly being left behind in favor of more agile-based methods.

Lengthy, paper-based project artifacts take significant time and effort to both generate and consume. Research has also shown that information presented in text-based formats is ineffective and inefficient. In fact, several supporting statistics exploring this concept indicate that, in order for information to be conveyed most efficiently, it needs to be visual. According to insightinformation.net, for example, the human eye can see visual patterns 65,000 times faster on a picture than in tabular form. And quintagroup.com claims 95% of all information is perceived through the eyes.

These facts have led to the creation of a new niche within the project management community known as "Visual Project Management." When it comes to improving project communication and collaboration, as well as visualizing processes, work flows and risks, visual project management has emerged as one of the best new methods for leading and managing projects.

The key benefit of this new approach is speed, as critical project information can be produced, replicated and digested in more effective and efficient ways. Taking this new approach also provides additional, distinct benefits to project managers, team members and, most importantly, key stakeholders:

- The status of project planning, execution, monitoring and control activities are available in a single, at-a-glance and easy to understand view
- Improves clarity, visibility and understanding of the scope and overall operational plan of the project effort
- Resource allocations, or over-allocations, across the project, or multiple projects, are clearly visible
- Impacts of changes to the scope, plan, priority or resource allocations are available in real-time
- Information is delivered in such a way that anyone can consume it at a time, place and manner that is convenient to them

Today's project manager has more to manage than just project scope, deliverables, communications and teams. They are also expected to manage large volumes of project-related data. And the expectation goes beyond just managing the data. It extends into creating great visualizations that allow stakeholders to fully digest that large volume of data in a manner that is quick, effective and clear. They are also expected to serve as facilitators in the use of visual thinking tools as a method for working through project issues, risks and problems. These new expectations require new skills. The era of multi-page, text-based project status reporting is over. The era of visual project management is here. **Time to "skill up!"**

About The Author

Paul R. Williams has over twenty years of project, program & portfolio management leadership experience with information technology, innovation management and strategic business initiatives in the investment, banking, insurance, legal, manufacturing and professional services industries. Mr. Williams is recognized as one of the pioneers of 'Visual Project Management,' a revolutionary new approach for leveraging visual thinking and communication strategies in project management practice. He has been featured in a number of worldwide publications including three appearances in PM Network, the official monthly periodical of the Project Management Institute, is the author of three books on innovation and project management, and is a frequent speaker on project and innovation management topics at conferences and media events across the United States.

Through his project and innovation management professional services firm, Think For A Change, LLC., Mr. Williams delivers educational, thought-leadership, coaching and consultation capabilities in the following areas:

PMO Management Services:
- Transitional PMO Leadership
- Traditional PMO Formation and Restructuring
- Alternative PM Governance Structures
- PMO Effectiveness Assessments
- Project Portfolio Financial Management

Executive Coaching Services:
- Project Management Governance
- Project Portfolio Management
- Innovation Management

Specialty Services:
- Visual Project Management Concepts
- War Room/Idea Center Design Services
- Keynote and Other Presentation Services

Professional Development Services:
- Project Management Simulations
- Innovation Management Training

In addition to his consultation work through Think For A Change, LLC., Paul R. Williams also serves as the Leader of Project Management for Plan Administrators, Inc. (PAi), and in that role is responsible for the leadership of the project portfolio management function at PAi including the integration of project management processes with SDLC and Agile execution approaches, oversight of a portfolio-based strategic project roadmap and accountability for a phase-gated project cost/benefit governance system.

Bibliography

Book-Based Resources:

A Project Guide to UX Design, by Russ Unger and Carolyn Chandler, New Riders, 2012

Agile Product Management with Scrum: Creating Products that Customers Love, by Roman Pichler, Addison-Wesley Professional, 2010

Agile Project Management with Scrum, by Ken Schwaber and Mike Beedle, Prentice Hall, 2001

Blah, Blah, Blah: What to Do When Words Don't Work, by Dan Roam, Penguin Group, 2013

Business Process Mapping: Improving Customer Satisfaction, by Mike J. Jacka and Paulette J. Keller, John Wiley & Sons, 2011

Cool Infographics: Effective Communication with Data Visualization and Design, by Randy Krum, Wiley, 2013

Earned Value Implementation Guide, by multiple authors from the Defense Contract Management Agency, DAU, 2006

Earned Value Project Management, Fourth Edition, by Quentin Fleming, Project Management Institute, 2010

Effective FMEAs, by Carl Carlson, Wiley, 2012

Envisioning Information, by Edward R. Tufte, Graphics Press, 1990

Essential Scrum: A Practical Guide to the Most Popular Agile Process, by Kenneth Rubin, Addison-Wesley Professional, 2012

Experiences in Visual Thinking, by Robert H. McKim, Brooks/Cole Publishing Co., 1972

Exploring Storyboarding, by Wendy Tumminello, Cengage Learning, 2004

Gamestorming: A Playbook for Innovators, Rulebreakers and Changemakers, by Dave Gray and Sunni Brown, O'Reilly Media, 2010

Gamification At Work: Designing Engaging Business Software, by Janaki Kumar and Mario Herger, Interaction-Design.org, 2013

Gamify: How Gamification Motivates People to Do Extraordinary Things, by Brian Burke, Bibliomotion, 2014

Infographics: Designing & Visualizing Data, by Wang Shaqiang, Promopress, 2014

Infographics: The Power of Visual Storytelling, by Jason Lankow, Josh Richie and Ross Crooks, Wiley, 2012

Information Dashboard Design: The Effective Visual Communication of Data, by Stephen Few, O'Reilly Media, 2006

Information Graphics: A Comprehensive Illustrated Reference, by Robert L. Harris, Oxford University Press, 1999

Kanban: Successful Evolutionary Change for Your Technology Business, by David J. Anderson, Blue Hole Press, 2010

Lean from the Trenches: Managing Large-Scale Projects with Kanban, by Henrik Kniberg, Pragmatic Bookshelf, 2011

Making Thinking Visible, by Ron Ritchhart, Mark Church and Karin Morrison, Jossey-Bass, 2011

Mapping Inner Space: Learning and Teaching Visual Mapping, by Nancy Margulies and Nusa Maal, Corwin, 2001

Mind Mapping for Dummies, by Florian Rustler, For Dummies Publishing, 2012

Modern Mind Mapping for Smarter Thinking, by Tony Buzan, Proactive Thinking, 2012

Object-Oriented Software Engineering - A Use Case Driven Approach, by Ivar Jacobson, M. Christerson, P. Jonsson and G. Övergaard, Addison-Wesley, 1992

Performance Dashboards: Measuring, Monitoring and Managing Your Business, by Wayne Eckerson, Wiley, 2010

Personal Kanban: Mapping Work | Navigating Life, by Tonianne DeMaria Barry and Jim Benson, CreateSpace, 2011

Planning and Road Mapping Technological Innovations: Cases and Tools, by Tugrul Daim and Melinda Pizarro, Springer, 2014

Practice Standard for Earned Value Management, by multiple authors from the Project Management Institute, Project Management Institute, 2005

Process Mapping, Process Improvement and Process Management, by Dan Madison, Paton Press, 2005

Professional Storyboarding: Rules of Thumb, by Anson Jew, Focal Press, 2013

Project Management Metrics, KPIs and Dashboards: A Guide to Measuring and Monitoring Project Performance, by Harold Kerzner, Wiley, 2013

Project Management Simulation with Project Team Builder (PTB), by Avraham Shtub, Springer, 2012

Project Management Using Earned Value, by Gary Humphreys, Humphreys and Associates, 2001

Road Mapping for Strategy and Innovation: Aligning Technology and Markets in a Dynamic World, by Robert Phaal and Clare Farrukh, Univ. of Cambridge Inst. For Mfg, 2010

Root Cause Analysis Handbook, by multiple authors at ABS Consulting, Rothstein Associates, 2008

Root Cause Analysis: A Tool for Total Quality Management, by Paul F. Wilson, Larry D. Dell and Gaylord F. Anderson, ASQ Quality Press, 1993

Root Cause Analysis: The Core of Problem Solving and Corrective Action, by Duke Okes, ASQ Quality Press, 2009

Show and Tell: How Everybody Can Make Extraordinary Presentations, by Dan Roam, Penguin Group, 2014

Show Me The Numbers: Designing Tables and Graphs to Enlighten, by Stephen Few, Analytics Press, 2012

Social Media for Project Managers, by Elizabeth Harrin, Project Management Institute, 2010

Storyboarding Essentials, by David Rousseau and Benjamin Phillips, Watson-Guptill, 2013

Technology Road Mapping for Strategy and Innovation: Charting the Route to Success, by Martin Moehrle, Ralf Isenmann and Robert Phaal, Springer, 2013

The Art of Social Media: Power Tips for Power Users, by Guy Kawasaki and Peg Fitzpatrick, Portfolio Hardcover, 2014

The ASQ Pocket Guide to Root Cause Analysis, by Bjorn Andersen and Tom Fagerhaug, ASQ Quality Press, 2013

The Back of the Napkin, by Dan Roam, Penguin Group, 2009

The Basics of Process Mapping, by Robert Damelio, Productivity Press, 2011

The Checklist Manifesto: How to Get Things Right, by Atul Gawande, Metropolitan Books, 2009

The Doodle Revolution: Unlock the Power to Think Differently, by Sunni Brown, Portfolio Hardcover, 2014

The Mind Map Book, by Tony Buzan, BBC Books, 1995

The Mind Map Book: How to Use Radiant Thinking to Maximize Your Brain's Untapped Potential, by Tony Buzan, Plume, 1996

The New One-Page Project Manager: Communicate and Manage Any Project with A Single Sheet of Paper, by Clark Campbell and Mick Campbell, Wiley, 2012

The Power of Infographics: Using Pictures to Communicate and Connect with Your Audience, by Mark Smiciklas, Que Publishing, 2012

The Sketchnote Handbook: The Illustrated Guide to Visual Note-Taking, by Mike Rohde, Peachpit Press, 2012

The Toyota Way, by Jeffrey Liker, McGraw-Hill, 2004

The Ultimate Book of Mind Maps, by Tony Buzan, Thorsons Publishers, 2006

The Virtual Worlds Handbook: How to Use SecondLife® and Other 3D Virtual Environments, by Elizabeth Hodge, Sharon Collins and Tracy Giordano, Jones & Bartlett Learning, 2009

The Visual Display of Quantitative Information, by Edward R. Tufte, Graphics Press, 2001

Unfolding the Napkin, by Dan Roam, Penguin Group, 2009

Visual Communication: Images with Messages, by Paul Martin Lester, Cengage Learning, 2013

Visual Explanations: Image and Quantities, Evidence and Narrative, by Edward R. Tufte, Graphics Press, 1997

Visual Leaders: New Tools for Visioning, Management and Organizational Change, by David Sibbet, Wiley, 2012

Visual Meetings: How Graphics, Sticky Notes and Idea Mapping Can Transform Group Productivity, by David Sibbet, Wiley, 2010

Visual Mojo, by Lynne Cazaly, Self-Published, 2014

Visual Teams: Graphic Tools for Commitment, Innovation and High Performance, by Davis Sibbet, Wiley, 2011

Visual Thinking, by Rudolph Arnheim, University of California Press, 1969

Visual Tools for Transforming Information Into Knowledge, by David Heyrle, Corwin, 2008

Visualize This: The FlowingData Guide to Design, Visualization and Statistics, by Nathan Yau, Wiley, 2011

Wireframing Essentials, by Matthew Hamm, Packt Publishing, 2014

Writing Effective Use Cases, by Alistair Cockburn, Addison-Wesley, 2001

Web-Based Resources:

American Society for Quality (ASQ), www.asq.org

Association for Project Management (UK), www.apm.org.uk

Beginner's Guide to Wireframing, bit.ly/1spBk2k (case sensitive)

Charting (Wikipedia), en.wikipedia.org/wiki/Chart

Cool Infographics Blog, www.coolinfographics.com

Creative Commons Search Engine, search.creativecommons.org

Dashboard Simulations, dashboardsimulations.com

David J. Anderson & Associates, www.djaa.com

Dimensional Insight Dashboard Design 101, www.dimins.com

Doodle (Wikipedia), en.wikipedia.org/wiki/Doodle

Earned Value (Wikipedia), en.wikipedia.org/wiki/Earned_value_management

Gamification (Wikipedia), en.wikipedia.com/wiki/Gamification

Gamification.org, badgeville.com/wiki

Google Image Search for Project Dashboard Examples, images.google.com

Humpreys & Associates, www.humpreys-assoc.com/evms

Image Think, http://www.imagethink.net, Nora Herting and Heather Willems

Infographic (Wikipedia), en.wikipedia.org/wiki/Infographic

Infographic Database, infographicdatabase.com

Ivar Jacobson International (Use Cases), www.ivarjacobson.com

Mind Map (Wikipedia), http://en.wikipedia.org/wiki/Mind_map

Mountain Goat Software, www.mountaingoatsoftware.com

One-Page Project Manager (Resources), www.oppmi.com

OpenLearn Works, www.open.edu (search diagrams, charts and graphs)

Orion Development Group, www.odgroup.com/articles/map-process/

Personal Kanban, www.personalkanban.com

Process Excellence Network, www.processExcellencenetwork.com

Process Mapping (Wikipedia), wikipedia.org/wiki/Business_process_mapping

Project Management Institute, www.pmi.org

Root Cause Analysis (Wikipedia), wikipedia.org/wiki/root_cause_analysis

Scrum Alliance, www.scrumalliance.org

Scrum Guides, www.scrumguides.com

Scrum.org, www.scrum.org

SimStudios, simstudios.com

Sketching (Wikipedia), en.wikipedia.org/wiki/Sketch_(drawing)

Sketching At Work, www.sketchingatwork.com/index.php/en/

Storyboard (Wikipedia), wikipedia.org/wiki/Storyboard

The Data Visualization Catalogue, www.datavizcatalogue.com

The Mind Mapping Software Blog, http://mindmappingsoftwareblog.com, Chuck Frey

ThinkBuzan, www.thinkbuzan.com

Tony Buzan, www.tonybuzan.com

Toyota Global – Just-in-Time & Kanban, bit.ly/XEjBZl (case sensitive)

Univ. of Houston, Education, tinyurl.com/lfobbwa

US DoD EVM Division, www.acq.osd.mil/evm

Use Case (Wikipedia), en.wikipedia.org/wiki/Use_case

Visual Literacy (Periodic Table of Visualization Methods), http://visual-literacy.org

Visual Literacy Guide, bit.ly/IX1bvI (case senstive)

Visual Literacy Project, bit.ly/IX1bvI

Visual Management Blog, www.xqa.com.ar/visualmanagement/

Visual Thinking Magic, http://www.visualthinkingmagic.com, Adam Sicinski.

VizThink, www.vizthink.com

Wireframe (Wikipedia), en.wikipedia.org/wiki/Website_wireframe

Wireframe Showcase, www.wireframeshowcase.com

Endnotes

[2] Beck, Kent; et al. (2001). "*Manifesto for Agile Software Development*". Agile Alliance. Retrieved 14 June 2010.

[3] Tufte, Edward (1983). *The Visual Display of Quantitative Information*. Cheshire, Connecticut: Graphics Press.

[4] http://en.wikipedia.org/wiki/Informational_graphics

[5] http://en.wikipedia.org/wiki/Visual_literacy

[6] http://en.wikipedia.org/wiki/Exploratory_data_analysis

[7] Deza, M.; Deza, E. (2009), *Encyclopedia of Distances*, Springer-Verlag,

[8] Medina, John (2009). *Brain Rules*. Pear Press.

[9] http://simplybrainy.com/wp-content/uploads/2011/01/2008-Int-Vis-Other-Senses-All-Illustrations.pdf

[10] Fixot, R. S.; American Journal of Ophthamology, 1957 Aug.

[11] Cunningham, Glennis Edge (Ph.D.) (2005). *Mindmapping: Its Effects on Student Achievement in High School Biology*. The University of Texas at Austin

[12] Holland, Brian, Holland, Lynda and Davies, Jenny (2004). "An investigation into the concept of mind mapping and the use of mind mapping software to support and improve student academic performance"

[13] Farrand, P.; Hussain, F.; Hennessy, E. (2002). "The efficacy of the mind map study technique". *Medical Education* **36** (5): 426–431

[14] http://www.tonybuzan.com/about/mind-mapping/

[15] http://thinkbuzan.com/how-to-mind-map/

[16] XMind Project Template posted for unrestricted, shared use via www.armerkater.de

[17] http://en.wikipedia.org/wiki/Business_process_mapping

[18] Jacka, J. Mike & Keller, Paulette J. (2011), *Business Process Mapping: Improving Customer Satisfaction*. John Wiley & Sons.

[19] Finch, Christopher. (2011), *The Art of Walt Disney*. Harry N. Abrams.

[20] http://en.wikipedia.org/wiki/Storyboard

[21] Wilson, Paul F.; Dell, Larry D.; Anderson, Gaylord F. (1993). *Root Cause Analysis: A Tool for Total Quality Management*. Milwaukee, Wisconsin: ASQ Quality Press. pp. 8–17.

[22] http://en.wikipedia.org/wiki/Ishikawa_diagram

[23] http://en.wikipedia.org/wiki/Failure_mode_and_effects_analysis

[24] Cary Jensen, Loy Anderson (1992). *Harvard graphics 3: the complete reference*. Osborne McGraw-Hill p.413

[25] H.L. Gantt, (1910) *Work, Wages and Profit*, published by *The Engineering Magazine*, New York,; republished as *Work, Wages and Profits*, (1974) Easton, Pennsylvania, Hive Publishing Company

[26] Peter W. G. Morris, Thomas Telford (1994), *The Management of Projects*, Google Print, p.18

[27] Wallace Clark and Henry Gantt (1922) *The Gantt chart, a working tool of management*. New York, Ronald Press.

[28] Malcolm, D. G., J. H. Roseboom, C. E. Clark, W. Fazar *Application of a Technique for Research and Development Program Evaluation* OPERATIONS RESEARCH Vol. 7, No. 5, September–October 1959, pp. 646–669

[29] http://www.danroam.com/the-back-of-the-napkin/

[30] Jacobson Ivar, Christerson M., Jonsson P., Övergaard G., (1992) *Object-Oriented Software Engineering - A Use Case Driven Approach*, Addison-Wesley

[31] Project Management Institute (2013) *A Guide to the Project Management Body of Knowledge (PMBOK Guide) – Fifth Edition*, Project Management Institute, pg. 217

[32] Defense Systems Management College (1997). *Earned Value Management Textbook*. Defense Systems Management College. Chapter 2

[33] http://sopheon.wpengine.netdna-cdn.com/wp-content/uploads/WhitePaper-Petrick-RoadmappingReferenceGuide.pdf

[34] http://www.globalnpsolutions.com/services/npd-resources/white-papers/roadmapping-101/conclusion/

[35] http://en.wikipedia.org/wiki/Kanban

[36] http://www.djaa.com/

[37] http://en.wikipedia.org/wiki/Kanban_(development)

[38] http://en.wikipedia.org/wiki/Little's_law

[39] http://www.leankit.com

[40] http://ja.wikipedia.org/wiki/lean_kanban

[41] http://agilemanifesto.org/

[42] http://en.wikipedia.org/wiki/Agile_software_development

[43] http://www.mountaingoatsoftware.com/agile/scrum/task-boards

[44] http://usatoday30.usatoday.com/news/snapshot.htm or *USA Today* print edition

[45] http://commons.wikimedia.org/wiki/File:Internet_Minute_Infographic.jpg

[46] https://www.smartgrid.gov/recovery_act/news/infographic_salt_river_project

[47] Original source: http://www.knowledgetree.com; Cited source: http://visual.ly/document-management-software-for-small-and-medium-businesses-8-steps-to-success-infographic

[48] Lisa Covi, Judith Olson and Elena Rocco, *A Room of Your Own: What Do We Learn About Support of Teamwork from Assessing Teams in Dedicated Project Rooms?*, Collaboratory for Research on Electronic Work, Univ. of Michigan, pp. 53-65;

[49] Steven M. Shaker, *Lessons Learned from War Room Designs and Implementations*, 2002 United States Department of Defense Command and Control Research and Technology Symposium; http://www.dodccrp.org/events/2002_CCRTS/Tracks/pdf/057.PDF

[50] Mike Eccles, Joanne Smith, Maureen Tanner, Jean-Paul Van Belle and Stephan van der Watt, *The Impact of Collocation on the Effectiveness of Agile in Development Teams*, International Business Information Management Association Journal, Vol. 2010, Article ID: 959194

[51] The Semantic CMS Community, IKS Semantic Engine Hackathon War Room, March 2010

[52] Time to Think, Genesis Grant Program, solutions.3m.com/innovation/en_US/stories/time-to-think

[53] United Kingdom Government Digital Service, Project Status Board

[54] DEC Worldwide Networking Exhibit by Phil Manker via Flickr

[55] Kaztec Engineering Project Showcase, 3rd Practical Nigerian Content Exhibition, Edwin Ndukwde

[56] 3M Innovation Center – Dubai, UAE: solutions.3m.com/innovation

[57] DuPont Innovation Center – Moscow, Russia: www.dupont.com/corporate-functions/our-approach/science/innovation-centers.html

[58] Gawande, Atul (2009), *The Checklist Manifesto: How To Get Things Right*, Metropolitan Books

[59] Panic Status Board is a trademark of Panic, Inc.

[60] Willy-Peter Schaub, Willy's Reflections – Visual Studio ALM Rangers Blog; via MSDN Blogs: blogs.msdn.com/b/willy-peter_schaub/

[61] Via lifehacker.com/5489288/staying-motivated-at-work-with-a-status-board, with further attribution to original content creator, Panic Software: www.panic.com/blog/2010/03/the-panic-status-board/ (*see note 58 – Panic Status Board is a trademark of Panic, Inc.*)

[62] "State of the media: The social media report 2012". Featured Insights, Global, Media + Entertainment. Nielsen. Retrieved 9 December 2012. and "The U.S. Digital Consumer Report". 2014-10-02. Retrieved 2014-11-25. www.nielsen.com/us/en/insights/reports/2014/the-us-digital-consumer-report.html

[63] The Conversation Prism v4.0, Brian Solis, Jesse Thomas and JESS3, conversationprism.com

[64] Based on a presentation of findings at an October 31st, 2012 event sponsored by the Thames Valley Branch of the United Kingdom-based, Association of Project Management

[65] McGonigal, Jane (2011), Reality Is Broken: Why Games Make Us Better and How They Change the World, Penguin Press

[66] Based on a presentation by M2 Research at the 2011 Gamification Summit in New York City

[67] Image courtesy of QueSocial; www.quesocial.com

[68] Image courtesy of SupercellMedia; www.supercellmedia.com/gamification-in-ecommerce

[69] Screen shot courtesy of SimulTrain, STS Sauter Training & Simulation SA, Lausanne, Switzerland; www.simultrain.com

Personal Notes